THE GREEN AISLE'S
HEALTHY INDULGENCE

More Than 75 Guilt-Free, All-Natural Recipes to Help You Lose Weight and Feel Great

MICHELLE SAVAGE

Skyhorse Publishing

The information given here is designed to help you make informed decisions about your health. It is not intended to replace the advice of a qualified health professional. If you have a condition that requires care, please seek treatment with your healthcare provider.

Skyhorse Publishing books may be purchased in bulk at special discounts for sales promotion, corporate gifts, fund-raising, or educational purposes. Special editions can also be created to specifications. For details, contact the Special Sales Department, Skyhorse Publishing, 307 West 36th Street, 11th Floor, New York, NY 10018 or info@skyhorsepublishing.com.

Skyhorse® and Skyhorse Publishing® are registered trademarks of Skyhorse Publishing, Inc.®, a Delaware corporation.

Visit our website at www.skyhorsepublishing.com.

10 9 8 7 6 5 4 3 2 1

Library of Congress Cataloging-in-Publication Data is available on file.

Cover design by Jane Sheppard

Cover photos provided by Shutterstock, Dreamstime, and Kenny Kaneshiro from CameraShock Photography

Print ISBN: 978-1-63450-710-3

Ebook ISBN: 978-1-63450-711-0

Printed in China

Contents

Indulgence

Where Food Brings Us Together

If you have a pure food *Indulgence* in mind, enjoy an intimate, relaxed dining experience that offers a variety of flavors.

Through this cookbook, you'll experience a memorable journey across the globe with every bite: Hawaiian Furikake Salmon, Israeli Shakshouka, Russian Borscht, Taste of Tuscany, Greek Pizza, Fancy Falafels, Jambalaya, Irish Brisket & Cabbage, Thai Shrimp Soup, Bunny Rabbit Sushi, Margo's Armenian Dolma, Smoked Apple Pulled Pork Tostadas, to name a few. Oh, not to mention these heavenly desserts: Coconut Key Lime Pie, Blueberry Mousse, Magic Shell Coconut Cream Pie Pops, and more—over 100 delectable recipes to choose from.

Indulgence features delicious dishes *without* refined sugars, artificial sweeteners, flavor enhancers, and the all-too-hidden processed foods containing GMOs or other foods known to cause health concerns. It's specifically designed to fuel your body with whole organic and natural ingredients from the time you wake up to the time you go to bed. What an all-inclusive cookbook for you, your family, and your guests.

When it comes to food, everybody has a different preference. Whether you like to walk in the garden, swim under the sea, or visit the lion's den, you'll find delicious options down to the finest details in these recipes.

In this cookbook, you won't find crazy diets that leave you starving or counting calories, and you won't be told to spend money on the latest weight-loss fad. Instead, you'll be inspired by Chef Michelle's tasty international and seasonal creations—all designed for sharing and enjoying.

Bon Appétit!

Author's Notes

Quality is Key

Choose to cook meals using fresh herbs and produce that are in season and buy the highest quality items you can find: organic produce, cage-free organic eggs, wild-caught seafood, and grass-fed meat including beef, chicken, and pork.

Don't be shy to ask your local butchers about the quality of seafood and meats. That's what they're there for! Request the cuts and thickness you desire; it won't cost a penny more.

Read Before Prep

Before attempting to create these delectable dishes, always take time to read through the ingredient list and directions carefully. Gather all ingredients and cooking equipment ahead of starting to cook. This is crucial; any starts and stops can slow you down. If you forget an important detail or key ingredient, you may render your dish less than desirable.

Tackle a Timeline

Prep whatever you can before starting to cook. Check for meals that require ingredients found in the Sauces, Dips & More section: Red Pepper Paste, Tzatziki Dipping Sauce, Homemade Sour Cream, or Toasted Honey Peanut Butter. This section is specifically designed to bring whole foods to your table the way nature intended and eliminate processed items that can contain unwanted preservatives.

Food Intolerances

While oats are naturally gluten-free, some companies package oats in a facility that also processes gluten products. If you have a gluten intolerance, be sure to buy gluten-free oats to avoid cross-contamination.

Throughout this book, each recipe is labeled with a symbol: Vegan, Vegetarian, Gluten-Free, Dairy-Free, Paleo, and "-opt" for optional suggestions.

Tzatziki Dipping Sauce and Homemade Sour Cream contain a cultured dairy kefir and are not vegan, but you can substitute homemade coconut milk yogurt. You'll find the recipe for it in the Sauces, Dips & More section.

Fine Balsamic Vinegar

Want to turn an ordinary meal into a gourmet cuisine right in your own kitchen? Fine balsamic elixirs, thick as molasses and barrel-aged to perfection, can make you wonder where that "ahhh" flavor is coming from. Add flavorful notes of fig, cranberry, strawberry, and rustic woody and fine port aromas.

Balsamic vinegars and cold-pressed oils used in this book come from the Olive Oil Pantry and can be purchased online at www.theoliveoilpantry.com.

Herbs & Spice Blends

Did you know that harmful toxins might be lurking in your spice cabinet? Many conventional spices have ingredients using fillers, flow agents, and preservatives. These might include (but are not limited to): salt, anti-caking agents, artificial colors and artificial flavors, and MSG (monosodium glutamate).

Therefore, always buy organic herbs and spices. When you do, your culinary creations will benefit from enhanced flavor and nourish your new lifestyle. Herbs and spice blends used in this book are from Spicely Organics, where you will find Adobo, Mediterranean, and more. This company does not use GMOs, MSG, fillers, sweeteners, or irradiation. Its products are kosher, vegan, and gluten-free. You can buy Spicely Organics spice blends at www.spicely.com.

Special Asterisks

Throughout the recipes, you will see an asterisk symbol * to guide you to special notes at the end of a recipe. These notes indicate where to purchase items, what ingredients you can substitute, or where you can create homemade recipes for ridiculously easy and deliciously wholesome condiments: Coconut Milk Yogurt, Salsa, Thai Peanut Sauce. They will keep your dishes close to what nature intended to sustain a healthy lifestyle!

Freezer Tips

Tired of throwing away citrus fruits when you can't get around to using them before they turn into hockey pucks? Using a handy citrus juicer, extract the juice from lemons, limes, oranges, and other fruits, then pour them into ice cube trays to freeze. They can readily be defrosted to have on hand. You can also drop them into your daily water to balance the pH and boost your immune system.

Be on the look-out for more notes, tips, and tricks throughout the text!

ALKALIZING INFUSIONS

Detox Tea

Yields 1 serving

Lil' bit of detox tea will do wonders for your body. Ginger soothes the tummy and gets your metabolism flowing, while lemon will alkalize and balance your body's pH—two incredible detoxifiers working in tandem to flush out toxins!

Ingredients
8–10 ounces (1¼ cups) water
1 ginger root sliver, smashed
2 lemon slices

1 teaspoon honey*
Dash cayenne (optional)

Directions
While bringing the water to a rolling boil, smash the ginger sliver with the back of your knife and add it to a teacup, along with honey. Gently pour water over the top. Before adding lemon slices to your tea, give them a little hug to bring out the juices. Lay lemon slices over the water and enjoy.

*Vegan option: maple syrup, agave, or a couple stevia drops

Cranberry Ginger Tea

Yields 2 servings

Recipe inspired by my dear friend Jeannie Gagney.

Ingredients
16 ounces (2 cups) water
½ cup organic fresh cranberries
1 tablespoon fresh ginger, peeled and finely grated
3 star anise pieces
1 cinnamon stick (optional)
1 lemon, juiced
2 teaspoons honey, divided*

Directions
Slice each cranberry in half and toss them into a small saucepan along with water; bring to a boil and cook for 3 minutes. Add ginger, star anise, and cinnamon. Reduce heat, cover and simmer for 8 to 10 minutes. Strain liquid with two layers of cheesecloth or a fine mesh strainer into a glass mug. Squeeze in lemon juice and stir in honey.

---

*Vegan option: agave

Vegan

Vegetarian

Gluten-Free

Dairy-Free

Paleo

Fizzy Ginger Ale

Yields 2 servings

Ingredients
1 lemon, juiced
1 lime, juiced
2 tablespoons maple syrup
1 teaspoon Organic Ginger Juice by The Ginger People or 1 teaspoon ginger root, grated
12 ounces (1½ cups) Superior Club Soda by Q Drinks

Directions
Combine all ingredients in a shaker bottle, shake vigorously, and pour over ice; allow to settle a bit and enjoy.

Vegan   Vegetarian   Gluten-Free   Dairy-Free   Paleo

Lemongrass Infusion

Yields 2 servings

Lemongrass is incredibly healing due to its anti-inflammatory, anti-cancer, and anti-oxidant properties. It aids in detoxification by flushing toxins and accrued fats from the body, balances intestinal flora, and contains vitamin A, B1, B2, B3, B5, B6, folate, and vitamin C, along with many other essential minerals.

Ingredients

2 lemongrass stalks
16 ounces (2 cups) water

1 tablespoon lemon juice
6 golden raisins, smashed or 6 stevia drops

Directions

Slice the bottom and top ends of the lemongrass stalks and discard. Make a thin slice along each lemongrass stalk lengthwise. Peel the dry outer layers of tough skin and discard.

Cut approximately 10 small slivers from the bottom of each lemongrass stalk, mash with a mallet, and place in a large glass pitcher along with lemon, smashed raisins and/or stevia, the remaining lemongrass stalks, and water. Give it a lil' whirl; cover and refrigerate overnight to infuse. Enjoy the next day; do not consume the lemongrass stalks or pieces.

Rosemary Infusion

Yields 2 servings

Rosemary has a multitude of medicinal effects. It relieves abdominal pain, gout, calms the nerves, and alleviates fatigue and anxiety. It contains anti-inflammatory properties, destroys microorganisms, improves blood flow, and eliminates mind fog. It increases energy and acts as a natural antidepressant, revitalizing the body.

Ingredients
¼ green apple
¼ Pink Lady apple

4 fresh rosemary sprigs
6 drops stevia (optional)
16 ounces (2 cups) water

Directions
Slice apples into ⅛-inch slivers. Roll rosemary between your fingers to bring out the aroma. Place apple slices, rosemary, stevia, and water in a large glass pitcher and give it a lil' whirl; cover and refrigerate overnight. Enjoy the next day while munching on apple slices.

Tangerine Infusion

Yields 4 servings

Tangerine infusion is refreshing and sweet. Tangerines also contain iron, folate, potassium, and flavonoids, which prevent cancer growth and tumors. They are antioxidant-rich and neutralize free radicals, which are essential in red blood cell regeneration. They protect our precious hearts against disease and blood clots.

Ingredients
4 tangerines
1–2 small mint sprigs
24 ounces (3 cups) water

Directions
Slice tangerines into ⅛-inch slivers, and roll the mint leaves between your fingers to bring out the aroma. Give the tangerine slices a bit of a hug into a glass pitcher and then drop those cuties in. Add mint leaves, water, and refrigerate overnight. The next day, remove mint leaves and consume within 24 to 36 hours.

Vegan

Vegetarian

Gluten-Free

Dairy-Free

Paleo

Chili-Lemon Detox

Yields 2 servings

Ingredients
2 lemons, juiced (yields ¼ cup juice)
1 cup water
¼ teaspoon probiotic powder*

⅛–¼ teaspoon cayenne
1 tablespoon maple syrup

Directions
Blend all ingredients in a high speed blender for 5 to 10 seconds; enjoy immediately or store in the refrigerator. Make sure to give it a little shake before consuming.

---

*Solaray Multidophilus Powder (non-dairy, freeze-dried, 5 billion triple strain formula): keep this product stored in the refrigerator.

JUST JUICE

Vegan Vegetarian Gluten-Free Dairy-Free Paleo

Perfect Pear

Yields 1 serving

Pear is a perfect juice; not only does it taste refreshingly amazing, its water-soluble pectin will act as a soothing diuretic, cleansing the colon to get things moving regularly. Pair that puppy with some rehydrating celery juice to replenish phytonutrients, help with digestion, and prevent kidney stones.

Ingredients
2 pears
2 celery stalks
1 Persian or small cucumber

Directions
Wash produce, cut to fit inside your juicer, and let the juicing begin. Drink immediately. If pear juice sits too long, it will oxidize and the color and taste will change.

Vegan

Vegetarian

Gluten-Free

Dairy-Free

Paleo

Celery Kist

Yields 1 serving

Celery is used as a base for many juices due to its high water content. It is one of the most hydrating and alkalizing vegetables the body can use, creating a perfect pH harmony, along with vitamins A, B1, B2, B6, C, potassium, folic acid, calcium, magnesium, iron, and essential amino acids; now just flavor that up a bit with the kiss of a Cutie!

Ingredients
3 celery stalks
2 Cuties Clementines or 1 orange, peeled

Directions
Wash produce, cut to fit inside your juicer, and let the juicing begin.

Vegan   Vegetarian   Gluten-Free   Dairy-Free   Paleo

Kale-Tastic Twist

Yields 1 serving

Kale encourages the production of enzymes in the liver that detoxify cancer-causing chemicals. Sulforaphane is also contained in kale, which prevents cancer by shutting off the gene associated with promoting abnormal cells into cancer cells. Maybe you're not a big fan of kale, but with this recipe, you'll hardly know it's there.

Ingredients
1 lemon, juiced
2 cups kale*

1 apple, chopped, seeds removed
½ teaspoon fresh ginger

Directions
Squeeze the juice of 1 lemon in a glass and set aside. Place the remaining ingredients into juicer and let the juicing begin. Pour in lemon juice. Stir and enjoy.

---

*Baby kale can be substituted if you're introducing kale into your diet; it is softer and less bitter.

Vegan Vegetarian Gluten-Free Dairy-Free Paleo

Fruit Punch

Yields 1 serving

Suffering from a bit of ol' age-related arthritis or gout? Anthocyanins contained in cherries can offer relief from inflammatory flare-ups, and this anti-oxidant-rich, tiny little Bing can sure pack a punch. Cherries reduce cell damage by scavenging free radicals; you know, those little buggers that attack our stable molecules and disrupt our living cells. Bye-bye "Buggers."

Ingredients
1 cup fresh dark cherries, pitted*
1 apple, chopped, seeds removed

1 orange, peeled
1 celery stalk

Directions
Place all ingredients into a juicer and let the juicing begin. Pour over frozen pitted cherries or ice cubes, if desired.

---

*Pitted dark cherries can be purchased in the frozen aisle of your local market. Allow them to defrost before juicing.

SMOOTHIES

Happy Lizard

Yields 1–2 servings

Rich and nutty hemp hearts are an excellent source of protein, omega-3, and omega-6 fatty acids. They regulate metabolism, bone health, and are absolutely one of my go-to's for sprinkling on top salads, as an add-in for smoothies, an ice cream topper, or just about anything.

Maca is a natural libido enhancer, a Viagra alternative, combats aging, and allows the body to feel youthful and vibrant.

Ingredients
16 ounces (2 cups) unsweetened almond milk
2 tablespoons plant-based vanilla protein powder
1 tablespoon raw hulled hemp hearts
1 tablespoon Maca powder
1 cup spinach leaves

Directions
Blend all ingredients in a high speed blender for 45 seconds or until smooth.

Vegan-opt Vegetarian-opt Gluten-Free Dairy-Free-opt Paleo-opt

Greek Honeycrisp Apple Yogurt Smoothie

Yields 1 serving

Pro and *biota* = for life. Probiotics are an everyday essential bacteria of live organisms used to aid in reestablishing and balancing the microflora in the gut—essential for persons suffering from IBS symptoms. You may think bacteria are bad, but there are trillions of essential bacteria that our body already has and needs to boost immunity, guard against harmful bacteria, aid in the digestion of food, and keep our intestines healthy to help the system become stronger.

Ingredients
1 cup Greek Gods Plain Kefir*
1 rhubarb, diced
1 Honeycrisp apple, chopped, seeds removed

Directions
Place all ingredients in a high speed blender for 45 seconds or until smooth.

---

*Coconut Milk Yogurt can be substituted for those who have a strong dairy intolerance (see page 257).

Vegan

Vegetarian

Gluten-Free

Dairy-Free

Paleo

Fruity Pebbles & Milk

Yields 1 serving

Ingredients
1 Envy apple, juiced (yields approx. 8 ounces or 1 cup)
1 banana
1 cup almond milk
2 strawberries, hulled

Directions
Place all ingredients into a high speed blender and blend for 45 seconds or until creamy.

BREAKFAST

Alternative Options: SPROUTED GRAINS: Dave's Killer Bread, Manna Bread, Ezekiel 4:9 Sprouted Grain; Rudi's Sprouted Multigrain Bread; GLUTEN FREE: Nature's Path Super Chia Bread, Happy Campers Stompin' Good Seedy Buckwheat Molasses Bread, Food for Life Exotic Black Rice Bread

Double-Dipp'en Sundried Tomato Toast & Heavenly Yolks

Yields 1–2 servings

Ingredients

2 organic pasture-raised eggs
2 slices Dave's Killer Bread*

1 tablespoon Earth Balance Olive Oil
   Buttery Spread
2 tablespoons sun-dried tomato paste by
   Amore All Natural

Directions

Bring a pot of water to a rolling boil and gently lower eggs into the water with a ladle; reduce heat to simmer. Cook for 6 to 7 minutes, depending how you like your yolks (runny or firmer). While the eggs are simmering, prepare an ice bath (a large bowl filled with ice water).

Ladle cooked eggs into the ice bath; allow to sit for two minutes to stop the cooking process. Tap around the top edge of each egg and peel the cap, leaving an egg shell filled with heavenly yolk. Snuggle your eggs in an egg cup or cut-out egg carton. Toast bread, smear with butter and sun-dried tomato paste, and start double dipp'en.

---

*Dave's Killer Bread found in most local markets or online at daveskillerbread.com. *No* high fructose corn syrup, *no* artificial preservatives, *no* artificial ingredients.

Potato Fritters

Yields 2 servings

Ingredients

4 small Yukon Gold potatoes
¼–⅓ cup yellow onion, chopped
3 tablespoons unbleached organic flour*
⅛ teaspoon aluminum-free baking powder
1 organic pasture-raised egg
½ teaspoon nutritional yeast

¼ teaspoon salt
Dash pepper
2 teaspoons Earth Balance Olive Oil Buttery Spread for frying, divided
Garnish with fresh strawberries, mint, and Homemade Sour Cream (see page 261)

Directions

Cut potato into small 1-inch pieces and place them into a food processor. Pulse until the potatoes are small, like grains of rice; set aside in a bowl. Add onion to the food processor and chop into very small pieces, then add to potatoes. Toss in flour, baking powder, egg, nutritional yeast, sea salt, and pepper; mix thoroughly.

Preheat skillet over medium heat and add 1 teaspoon of butter; spread the melted butter around the skillet. Premeasure 1 tablespoon rounds for each scoop of fritter mix into your skillet and softly flatten each with the back end of the tablespoon. Cook approximately 3 to 4 minutes per side until crisp. Repeat the next batch with the remaining butter and fritter mix and serve piping hot with a dollop of sour cream, fresh mint, and strawberry or other fresh fruit.

---

*Gluten-free option: King Arthur Gluten-Free Multi-Purpose Flour or Bob's Red Mill Gluten Free All-Purpose Baking Flour

Vegetarian   Gluten-Free   Dairy-Free   Paleo

Oven Poached Eggs

Yields 2 servings

Ingredients

1 teaspoon Earth Balance Olive Oil
   Buttery Spread, divided
½ cup egg whites, divided
8–10 spinach leaves, divided

1 small vine-ripened tomato, cored and
   sliced into small wedges
2 organic pasture-raised eggs
Garnish with Dynamite Pico De Gallo
   (see page 263)

Directions

Grease two oven-safe glass bowls or ramekins with ½ teaspoon of butter in each. In each ramekin pour ¼ cup egg whites, half the spinach, and tomato wedges. Gently crack 1 egg into each bowl, and add the remaining spinach leaves.

In a medium-sized glass casserole dish, add water to fill approximately 1-inch high. Pour that measured water into a pot and bring to a boil. Add the water back to the glass casserole dish again and carefully place your two filled ramekins into the water-filled casserole dish. The water should raise to approximately half the height up the sides of the ramekins.

Place casserole dish on the bottom rack of a preheated oven at 375°F and cook for approximately 13 minutes, depending upon how well you would like your yolks cooked. Thirteen minutes is the perfect time for a poached egg. Gently remove with oven mitts and serve alone or topped with Dynamite Pico De Gallo.

Reese's Peanut Butter Cup Oats

Yields 1 serving

Ingredients

1 serving Old-Fashioned Oatmeal (see page 45)
1 tablespoon plant-based vanilla protein powder
1 tablespoon natural peanut butter or Toasted Honey Peanut Butter (see page 267)
1–2 additional tablespoons nut milk
1 tablespoon honey*

Directions

Follow the directions for Old-Fashioned Oatmeal. Ladle 1 cup of oats into a serving bowl and stir in vanilla protein powder, peanut butter, and desired nut milk. Top with drizzlette of honey or agave.

---

*Vegan option: agave

Old-Fashioned Oatmeal

Yields 2 servings

Do you soak your oats? Oats are not easily digestible and inhibit the release of nutrients until you soak them first to reduce the phytic acid, which can cause stomach upset and improper digestion.

Ingredients
1 cup whole rolled oats
2 cups water, plus ¾ cup water
2 tablespoons almond milk

Directions
Combine oats and 2 cups of water in a pot; soak overnight on your countertop for 12 to 24 hours. This will reduce the phytic acid and allow iron and other nutrients to be absorbed more readily. After soaking your oats, pour and drain them in a fine mesh strainer; rinse and drain thoroughly.

Return oats to the pot and add ¾ cup water; cook over medium heat and stir occasionally for approximately 5 minutes or until oats are to your desired consistency. For thinner oats, add an additional ¼ cup water while cooking.

Ladle a cup of oats into a serving bowl and stir in 2 tablespoons almond milk; top with your favorite garnish. Remaining oats can be stored in the refrigerator and eaten cold the next day or reheated on the stovetop with a few tablespoons of water. Garnish with Blueberry Jam (265), Peaches & Cream (49), or a Reese's Peanut Butter Cup (44).

Jammen Blueberry Oats

Yields 1 serving

Ingredients

1 serving Old-Fashioned Oatmeal (see page 45)
2–3 tablespoons Blueberry Jam (see page 265)
2–3 tablespoons almond milk
1–2 teaspoons sunflower seeds
Garnish with a few walnuts or pecans and fresh blueberries

Directions

Follow the directions for Old-Fashioned Oatmeal. Ladle 1 cup of oats into a serving bowl and stir in Blueberry Jam and almond milk. Top with sunflower seeds, nuts, and fresh blueberries. Be sure to make your Jammen Blueberry Toast (48) for dippen!

Jammen Blueberry Toast

Yields 1–2 servings

Ingredients
2 slices Dave's Killer Bread*
2 tablespoons GO VEGGIE Vegan Classic Plain Cream Cheese
2 tablespoons Blueberry Jam (see page 265)

Directions
Toast your favorite bread, slather with cream cheese and Blueberry Jam; dip in your Jammen Blueberry Oats (47) and devour.

Alternative Options: SPROUTED GRAINS: Dave's Killer Bread, Manna Bread, Ezekiel 4:9 Sprouted Grain; Rudi's Sprouted Multigrain Bread; GLUTEN FREE: Nature's Path Super Chia Bread, Happy Campers Stompin' Good Seedy Buckwheat Molasses Bread, Food for Life Exotic Black Rice Bread

---

*Dave's Killer Bread found in most local markets or online at daveskillerbread.com. *No* high fructose corn syrup, *no* artificial preservatives, *no* artificial ingredients.

Vegan Vegetarian Gluten-Free Dairy-Free

Peaches & Cream Oats

Yields 1 serving

Ingredients
1 serving Old-Fashioned Oatmeal (see page 45)
1 tablespoon plant-based vanilla protein powder
1 peach, sliced and pitted
1–2 additional tablespoons nut milk

Directions
Follow the directions for Old-Fashioned Oatmeal. Ladle 1 cup of oats into a serving bowl and stir in vanilla protein powder and desired nut milk. Top with peach slices.

Vegetarian-opt Gluten-Free Dairy-Free-opt Paleo

Mushroom & Spinach Frittata

Yields 4 servings

Ingredients

1 tablespoon Earth Balance Olive Oil
 Buttery Spread
10 organic pasture-raised eggs
¼ cup GO VEGGIE Vegan Classic Plain
 Cream Cheese
¼ cup red onion, diced
1 cup mushrooms, sliced
1 cup baby spinach

1 teaspoon Adobo seasoning
Pinch sea salt
½ teaspoon aluminum-free baking
 powder
¼ cup fresh Parmesan cheese, grated
 (optional)*
Garnish with Dynamite Pico De Gallo
 (see page 263)

Directions

Grease a cast iron skillet with butter, making sure to run the butter up the sides of the skillet; set aside. Lightly whisk eggs and cream cheese in a bowl; add onion, mushrooms, spinach, Adobo, sea salt, baking powder, and Parmesan. Blend gently and pour into the greased skillet.

Cook in a preheated oven at 350°F for 20 minutes until egg is cooked through. Top with Parmesan and cook a few additional minutes until cheese is melted. Remove from the oven with oven-safe mitts and cut into pie slices with a spatula. Serve warm with Dynamite Pico De Gallo.

---

*Dairy-free option: omit Parmesan cheese

Fruit & Granola Chia Parfait

Yields 1 serving

Ingredients

½ cup Greek Gods Plain Kefir*
¼ cup chia seeds
1 teaspoon agave
1½ cups rolled oats
3 tablespoons water
½ teaspoon alcohol-free vanilla extract

¼ cup maple syrup
¼ teaspoon cinnamon
1 tablespoon olive oil
Dash cardamom
2 strawberries, hulled and chopped
Handful blueberries

Directions

Combine kefir, chia seeds, and agave in a glass. Stir thoroughly and allow to thicken in the refrigerator for at least 15 minutes while making the granola.

To make granola: combine oats, water, vanilla, maple syrup, cinnamon, olive oil, and cardamom in a large bowl; squeeze with your hands to mix thoroughly. Spread mixture evenly onto a baking sheet and cook on a low rack at 275°F for 45 to 60 minutes, tossing once or twice during baking, until golden brown. Allow to cool a bit.

Now for the fun part; grab a pretty serving glass and add ¾ cup granola, then spoon the chilled chia, ¼ cup granola, and top with fruit. Leftover granola can be stored in a Mason jar in the cupboard or refrigerator for up to 2 weeks.

---

*Coconut Milk Yogurt can be substituted for those who have a strong dairy intolerance (see page 257).

Poached Egg & Asparagus

Yields 1 serving

Ingredients
1 organic pasture-raised egg
8 asparagus spears, tough ends removed
2 teaspoons white balsamic vinegar

Directions
Fill a small skillet with 2 inches of water and bring to a low boil. Add asparagus and poach for approximately 1½ to 2 minutes until fork-tender; remove asparagus and set aside on a serving plate, reserving skillet water.

Gently crack 1 egg into a small ramekin and set aside. Bring reserved skillet water back to a low boil, whirl in white balsamic vinegar, and gently pour the egg into the center of the swirling water. Use a slotted spoon to swirl the water around the outer portion of the egg to keep it intact; cook for 3 minutes.

Use a slotted spoon to gently lift the egg out of the water; allow the water to seep through the slots of the spoon and place the egg onto the asparagus.

Vegetarian Gluten-Free Dairy-Free Paleo

Israeli Shakshouka

Yields 2–4 servings

Ingredients

1 tablespoon Earth Balance Olive Oil
    Buttery Spread
¼ cup yellow onion, minced
2 large garlic cloves, minced
¼ teaspoon coriander seeds
4 large heirloom tomatoes
1 red bell pepper, diced
2 fresh parsley sprigs, chopped
1 whole bay leaf
½ teaspoon sea salt

½ teaspoon celery seed powder
½ teaspoon sage powder
½ teaspoon crushed red pepper flakes
1 teaspoon sweet paprika
3 organic pasture-raised eggs
Garnish with a pinch of Organic Greek,
    Organic Herbs De Provence, or
    Organic Vegetable Seasoning from
    Spicely Organics (optional)

Directions

Sauté garlic and onion in butter in a cast iron skillet for 5 minutes. During the sauté, place the coriander seeds into a plastic sandwich bag and roll over the top with a rolling pin to smash and release aroma; add to the skillet.

Chop tomatoes in a food processor or dice into small pieces and add to the skillet along with red bell pepper, parsley, bay leaf, sea salt, celery seed powder, sage powder, and crushed red pepper flakes. Bring to a low boil, cover, and reduce heat to simmer for 35 minutes.

The sauce should be bubbling slowly by this point and all the flavors infused; add sweet paprika and give it a little stir. Slowly crack eggs over the sauce, nestling them inside the veggies. Cover and simmer for 4 to 5 minutes and serve. Traditionally served with crunchy warm bread to mop up the sauce; great for lunch or dinner.

Vegetarian   Gluten-Free   Dairy-Free   Paleo

Egg White Omelet

Yields 1 serving

Ingredients
1 teaspoon Earth Balance Olive Oil Buttery Spread
1 cup egg whites, whisked
½–1 cup spinach, chopped
Pinch sea salt

Directions
Melt butter in small nonstick skillet over medium heat. Whisk spinach and sea salt with egg whites; pour over butter. Cook for a couple minutes until the whites start to become opaque, then fold whites in half once and cook for 30 seconds. Fold whites in half again and cook for a few more seconds until done.

Serve with freshly squeezed orange juice; the vitamin C in the orange juice will help the body absorb the iron in the spinach more readily.

Vegan Vegetarian Gluten-Free Dairy-Free

Breakfast Oven-Roasted Corn on the Cob

Yields 1–4 servings

Easy oven-roasted corn on the cob—no foil, no soaking, no boiling, no husking!

Ingredients
1–4 ears of organic corn on cob with husks
1–4 teaspoons Earth Balance Olive Oil Buttery Spread (optional)
1–4 pinches sea salt (optional)

Directions
Slice the large stalk at the end a bit, and trim excessive silk from the end of the corn on the cob just to make sure nothing will catch fire during the roast. Place corn on the cob with husks onto a baking sheet and roast in oven at 350°F for approximately 35 to 40 minutes. Remove from oven and allow to cool a bit; now the inner silk can easily be peeled back the husk. Enjoy al dente or add a touch of butter and a pinch of sea salt.

Berry Bowl

Yields 1 serving

Ingredients
½ cup strawberries, hulled and sliced
½ cup blueberries
¼ cup raw pecan pieces
8–12 ounces (1–1½ cups) almond milk
Dash cinnamon

Directions
Arrange fruit and pecans in a small bowl; top with almond milk and a shake of cinnamon. Use seasonal fresh fruit when available and pair with other types of nuts; apples and pecans, bananas with almond slivers, figs, and pistachios.

SNACKS

Cran-Apple Cookie Crisps

Yields 4 servings

Ingredients
5 dates, pitted
½ cup walnuts
1 Honeycrisp, Autumn Glory, or Envy apple, cored and seeds removed
1 tablespoon chia seeds
¼ cup dried cranberries
1 tablespoon macaroon coconut

Directions
Chop dates into tiny pieces and place in the food processor and pulse approximately 12 to 15 times. Add nuts and pulse until chopped into small pieces.

Chop apple into small ½-inch pieces and add to the food processor along with the chia seeds, cranberries, and macaroon coconut. Pulse until slightly chunky like grains of rice.

Scoop out mixture and layer evenly onto a cutting board. Use a ¼ measuring cup or other preferred round cookie cutter and gently press down to make little cookies. Scoop up cookie pieces with a spatula and layer onto a dehydrator tray; dehydrate at 115°F for 14 to 16 hours until crispy.

Vegan

Vegetarian

Gluten-Free

Dairy-Free

Celery Boat

Yields 2 servings

Ingredients
2 celery stalks
2 tablespoons Toasted Honey Peanut Butter (see page 267)
Small handful raisins, dried cherries, or dried cranberries

Directions
Remove the tough ends and leafy celery tops; discard or save for juicing. Cut celery stalks into desired bite sized pieces; fill with peanut butter and sprinkle preferred dried fruit on top.

Date Poppers

Yields 1 serving

Ingredients
3 Medjool dates
3 nuts of your choice: Naked Almonds (see page 69), walnuts, or macadamias

Directions
Slice the dates lengthwise, remove the seeds, and discard. Place preferred nut inside each date and squeeze the flesh of the date back together to enjoy your little candy treat.

Vegan

Vegetarian

Gluten-Free

Dairy-Free

Paleo

Naked Almonds

Yields 1–2 servings

Ingredients
½ cup almonds
3 cups water

Directions
Pour water in a pot and bring to a boil; remove the pot from the burner and add almonds. Allow to seep for 60 to 90 seconds while the casings loosen; strain and rinse.

Grab each almond from the end and give them a little squeeze. The casings will easily slip off. Snack on ¼ cup almonds per serving size, approximately a small handful. Be sure to chew them thoroughly for proper digestion.

Naked almonds can be used to make a sweet candy treat, Date Poppers (see page 67).

Almond casings can be reserved for Fluffy Almond Croutons (see page 71), a great soup or salad topper.

Vegan   Vegetarian   Gluten-Free-opt   Dairy-Free

Pizza Toasties

Yields 1 serving

Ingredients
1 sourdough bread slice*
1 teaspoon Earth Balance Olive Oil Buttery Spread
1 garlic clove, smashed
1½ teaspoons sun-dried tomato paste by Amore All Natural
3 green olives by Organic Divina, pitted and sliced

Directions
Toast sourdough slice in toaster and toast well, coat with butter and slather the smashed garlic clove over the top to spread the butter around, creating a hint of garlic flavor; discard garlic. Spread sundried tomato paste over the garlic butter and top with green olives.

Alternative Options: SPROUTED GRAINS: Dave's Killer Bread, Manna Bread, Ezekiel 4:9 Sprouted Grain; Rudi's Sprouted Multigrain Bread; GLUTEN FREE: Nature's Path Super Chia Bread, Happy Campers Stompin' Good Seedy Buckwheat Molasses Bread, Food for Life Exotic Black Rice Bread

---

*Best cut fresh from a large sourdough loaf

Fluffy Almond Croutons

Yields 1–2 servings

Ingredients
½ cup almond casings
¼ teaspoon olive oil
¼–½ teaspoon nutritional yeast
Pinch sea salt

Directions
Combine oil, nutritional yeast, and sea salt in a small bowl and gently mix in almond casings to coat well. Place casings onto a baking sheet and cook in a preheated oven at 350°F for 5 minutes. Remove from oven and allow to cool; store in a Mason jar in the cupboard until you're looking for a healthy light crunch to your soup or salad.

Autumn Applesauce

Yields 4 servings

Ingredients
6 Autumn Glory apples, peeled, cored, and chopped*
1½ cup water

Directions
Add apples and water to a crock pot and cook on high for 3½ hours; stir once or twice during cook time.

Allow apples to cool a bit and pour into a high speed blender or use a handheld mixer to blend until desired consistency. Place into Mason jars and store in the refrigerator.

Fun Add-In: Add a dash of cinnamon to the crock pot to spice up the flavors.

---

*A variety of apples can be substituted.

Zucchini Snaps

Yields 4 servings

Ingredients

1 zucchini
1 small Roma tomato
2 tablespoons GO VEGGIE Vegan Classic Plain Cream Cheese
2 parsley sprigs, plus a few leaves for garnish

Directions

Cut the ends of zucchini and discard. Slice zucchini and tomato into $\frac{1}{6}$-inch slices. A mandoline works best. Take 1 slice of zucchini and layer $\frac{1}{2}$ teaspoon cream cheese, 1 parsley leaf, 1 tomato slice, another parsley leaf, another layer of $\frac{1}{2}$ teaspoon cream cheese, and top with another slice of zucchini and parsley leaf.

Continue to layer the remaining ingredients until you have a bunch of Zucchini Snaps. Snack on two or three and store the remaining snaps in the refrigerator for the next time you get the munchies.

Avocado Festival

Yields 2 servings

Ingredients
1 avocado, halved and pitted
2 cherry tomatoes
2 blackberries
2 mandarin wedges
2 hazelnuts, chopped
2 mint leaves, chopped

Directions
Nestle tomato in the center of the avocado half, hug in a blackberry and mandarin; sprinkle hazelnuts and mint.

Vegan

Vegetarian

Gluten-Free

Dairy-Free

Paleo

Apples & Cinnamon Chips

Yields 2 servings

Ingredients
2 apples, your choice
1½ tablespoons cinnamon
1 tablespoon olive oil

Directions
Slice apples ⅛ inch or thinner. A mandoline works best. Discard seeds and stems. Place olive oil in a small bowl and cinnamon in another small bowl. Dip the tips of your fingers into the oil and slightly coat each side of the apple slices and sprinkle each slice with cinnamon.

   Layer each slice evenly on a dehydrator tray. Cook at 115°F for approximately 6 hours until crisp. Store apple cinnamon chips in a Mason jar with a lid in cupboard or refrigerator for up to 3 to 4 weeks.

Fun Add-In: Sprinkle a bit of peanut butter powder onto each apple slice before dehydrating.

Vegan   Vegetarian   Gluten-Free   Dairy-Free   Paleo

Nacho Cheeseless Kale Chips

Yields 2–4 servings

Ingredients

1 bunch kale
½ cup cashews
1 teaspoon chives
1 teaspoon olive oil
¼ red bell pepper
2 tablespoons organic low-sodium
    vegetable broth
⅛ teaspoon celery seed powder

⅛ teaspoon sweet paprika
⅛ teaspoon mustard powder
⅛ teaspoon cayenne
½ teaspoon lemon juice
2 slivers Anaheim pepper
1 teaspoon apple cider vinegar
1 teaspoon nutritional yeast
Dash sea salt

Directions

Remove large stems from kale, chop leaves into bite-sized pieces, and set aside in a large bowl. It should yield approximately 8 cups chopped.

To make your nacho cheese sauce, place all other ingredients into a high speed blender and purée until creamy. Drizzle sauce onto the kale and massage with your hands to soften the leaves. Mix thoroughly.

Spread nacho cheeseless kale onto a few dehydrator trays and dehydrate at 115°F overnight.

Vegan   Vegetarian   Gluten-Free   Dairy-Free   Paleo

Watercress Infusion

Yields 1 serving

Ingredients
¼ avocado
3 cherry tomatoes
1 tablespoon watercress leaves
1 teaspoon olive oil
Pinch sea salt and crushed peppercorn

Directions
Slice avocado lengthwise into 3 slices and place on a dish facing the same direction. Slice each tomato in half and carefully snuggle them upright in between each avocado slice. Drizzle with oil, watercress, sea salt, and peppercorn.

Superfood Granola

Yields 2–4 servings

Ingredients

1½ cups rolled oats
3 tablespoons water
½ teaspoon alcohol-free vanilla extract
¼ cup honey*
¼ teaspoon cinnamon
1 tablespoon olive oil

Dash cardamom
⅛ cup pepitas**
⅛ cup goji berries
⅛ cup sunflower seeds
⅛ cup raisins or cranberries or a
combination of both

Directions

Combine oats, water, vanilla, honey, cinnamon, olive oil, and cardamom in a large bowl; squeeze with your hands to mix thoroughly. Spread mixture onto a baking sheet and cook on a low rack at 275°F for 45 to 60 minutes, tossing once or twice during baking until golden brown. Allow to cool a bit.

Pour granola into a bowl, along with pepitas, goji berries, sunflower seeds, and raisins; toss and pour into a Mason jar with lid. Store in cupboard or refrigerator for 3 to 4 weeks.

*Vegan option: agave or maple syrup
**Pepitas are flat green pumpkin seeds.

LUNCH

Open Face Radish Sandwich

Yields 2 servings

Ingredients

2 slices Dave's Killer Bread*
2 teaspoons GO VEGGIE Vegan Classic Plain Cream Cheese
2–4 small butter lettuce leaves
2 radishes, sliced
2–4 cucumber slices
1–2 organic pasture-raised Boiled Eggs, sliced (see page 271)

Directions

Spread 1 teaspoon cream cheese on each slice of bread. Layer lettuce, cucumber, radish, and egg slices.

Fun Add-In: Top with red pepper flakes and pinch of sea salt.

Alternative Options: SPROUTED GRAINS: Dave's Killer Bread, Manna Bread, Ezekiel 4:9 Sprouted Grain; Rudi's Sprouted Multigrain Bread; GLUTEN FREE: Nature's Path Super Chia Bread, Happy Campers Stompin' Good Seedy Buckwheat Molasses Bread, Food for Life Exotic Black Rice Bread

---

*Dave's Killer Bread found in most local markets or online at daveskillerbread.com. *No* high fructose corn syrup, *no* artificial preservatives, *no* artificial ingredients.

Vegan Vegetarian Gluten-Free-opt Dairy-Free

Beet & Arugula Sandwich

Yields 2 servings

Ingredients

2 slices Dave's Killer Bread*
1 small beet
1 tablespoon GO VEGGIE Vegan Classic
   Plain Cream Cheese

½ avocado
⅓ cup arugula
Small handful pea shoots or sprouts

Directions

Slice beet into ⅛-inch slices. A mandoline works best. You will get approximately 5 to 7 slices. Steam the slices for 30 to 40 minutes until tender. Beets will stain so be careful while handling them. On one slice of bread, spread the cream cheese. Cut steamed beet slices into small squares and layer on top of the cream cheese, smashing it down with a fork.

With the avocado half in one hand, use a butter knife to make thin slices lengthwise down the avocado and scoop it out with a spoon. Layer slices on top of the beet, stack arugula, and toss some pea shoots in the mix. Top with another slice of bread, cut diagonally, and enjoy.

Alternative Options: SPROUTED GRAINS: Dave's Killer Bread, Manna Bread, Ezekiel 4:9 Sprouted Grain; Rudi's Sprouted Multigrain Bread; GLUTEN FREE: Nature's Path Super Chia Bread, Happy Campers Stompin' Good Seedy Buckwheat Molasses Bread, Food for Life Exotic Black Rice Bread

*Dave's Killer Bread found in most local markets or online at daveskillerbread.com. *No* high fructose corn syrup, *no* artificial preservatives, *no* artificial ingredients.

Stuffed Mushroom Bites

Yields 2–4 servings

Ingredients

¼ cup pecans
8 crimini mushrooms
1 tablespoon olive oil
1½ teaspoon of minced green onion
   whites
1 tablespoon organic low-sodium
   vegetable broth

1 tablespoon nutritional yeast
1 small garlic clove
1 teaspoon thyme
Dash cayenne
Dash sea salt
1 tablespoon fresh parsley, plus a few
   leaves for garnish

Directions

Place pecans into a food processor and pulse until pecans are the size of small rice grains. Remove stems from mushroom caps and place them into the food processor with all other ingredients except mushroom caps; pulse until thoroughly blended, but slightly chunky.

Spoon mixture into each mushroom cap and enjoy raw or toast for 10 minutes under a broiler and top with fresh parsley.

Bunny Rabbit Sushi

Yields 2–4 servings

Ingredients
2 nori sheets
4 carrots
½ avocado, sliced
¼ red and yellow bell pepper, sliced
½ teaspoon sesame seeds

Directions
Finely grate carrots until you have approximately 3 cups; set aside in a strainer.

Place one sheet of nori on a dry cutting board and apply a thin layer of grated carrot on ¾ of the nori sheet, leaving 1 inch of the nori sheet dry for sealing.

On the carrot end of the nori wrap, layer avocado and bell peppers; roll tightly with fingertips. Spread a thin layer of water on the dry nori end and continue wrapping to seal the roll; press gently.

Wet a sharp knife and cut the bunny sushi into desired thickness by slowly sliding the knife back and forth. Clean and dry residue off the knife between each slice. Arrange each slice on ends and sprinkle with sesame seeds.

Cabbage Patch Wrap

Yields 2 servings

Ingredients
2 butter lettuce or large lettuce leaves for wrap
2 ounces (approx. ¾ scant cup) red cabbage, sliver slices
2 ounces (approx. ¾ scant cup) green cabbage, sliver slices
½ carrot, sliced into thin matchsticks
4 tablespoons Tzatziki Dipping Sauce* (see page 255)
2 (6-inch) lengths kitchen twine

Directions
Slather 2 tablespoons of Tzatziki Dipping Sauce over the inside of each lettuce leaf; divide and layer green and red cabbage and carrots. Wrap tightly but gently; tie with kitchen twine and enjoy!

Feeling a little lazy? Use pre-mixed and pre-packaged tri-color coleslaw, which contains sliced green and red cabbage and carrots.

---

*Coconut Milk Yogurt can be substituted for those who have a strong dairy intolerance (257).

Vegan Vegetarian Gluten-Free Dairy-Free

Northern Bean Hummus

Yields 4 servings

Ingredients

1 cup great northern white beans
2½ cups water, plus 2 tablespoons water
1 teaspoon sea salt
2 garlic cloves, smashed

½ teaspoon cumin
⅓ cup olive oil, plus 1 tablespoon
1 teaspoon red wine vinegar
2 teaspoons lime juice

Directions

Rinse and remove debris from beans. Add beans, 2½ cups water, sea salt, garlic, and cumin to slow cooker and cook on high for 3½ to 4 hours or until beans are very soft. Allow to cool.

Place beans, ⅓ cup olive oil, red wine vinegar, 2 tablespoons water, and lime juice into a food processor or high speed blender and purée until you reach desired consistency. Scrape down the sides once or twice during purée. Scoop into a serving bowl and top with 1 tablespoon olive oil; stir slightly. Serve with veggies, toasted pita, sea salt pita chips, or slathered on toasted Dave's Killer Bread.

Next time try adding ½ teaspoon sweet or smoked paprika before puréeing to give it a little kick!

Pea Crostini

Yields 2–3 servings

Ingredients

1 cup organic peas, plus 2 tablespoons for garnish

1 tablespoon Earth Balance Olive Oil Buttery Spread, melted

6 slices sourdough baguette*

1 garlic clove

¼ teaspoon sea salt

½ teaspoon white balsamic vinegar

Dash cracked peppercorn

1 radish, sliced into ¹⁄₁₆-inch slivers

⅓ cup arugula mixed greens

1½ teaspoon olive oil

Pinch fresh grated Parmesan (optional)**

Directions

Cook peas and enough water to cover them in a small pot over medium-low heat for 5 minutes. Use a slotted spoon to scoop out peas and place them into a food processor; setting aside 2 tablespoons peas for garnish.

Slather butter among the baguette slices. Place on the barbecue butter side down for approximately 3 to 5 minutes until there are nice grill marks or place onto a baking sheet and broil for 5 minutes.

Smash the garlic clove with the large part of a cleaver and rub over the buttered side of each grilled baguette slice. Toss the smashed garlic piece into the food processor with the cooked peas, add sea salt, white balsamic vinegar, and peppercorn. Purée for approximately 30 to 40 seconds until creamy. Spread each baguette slice with pea purée and top with radish, arugula, and Parmesan. Garnish with remaining peas and drizzle each slice with a bit of olive oil.

---

*Gluten-free option: Nature's Path Super Chia Bread, Happy Campers Stompin' Good Seedy Buckwheat Molasses Bread, Food for Life Exotic Black Rice Bread

**Vegan and dairy-free option: omit Parmesan

Applewood Wild Salmon & Capers

Yields 2 servings

Ingredients

2 tablespoons GO VEGGIE Vegan Classic Plain Cream Cheese
2 large crispbread flax crackers*
8 thin cucumber slices
4–6 pieces of mixed greens or arugula
2 ounces smoked salmon
1 teaspoon capers by La Pedriza

Directions

Spread cream cheese on crackers, top with cucumber and lettuce. Remove salmon from packaging and separate, layer over lettuce, and top with capers.

---

*Gluten-free option: Le Pain des Fleurs Natural Quinoa Crispbread

Vegan

Vegetarian

Gluten-Free

Dairy-Free

Paleo

Yam & Cabbage Soup

Yields 2 servings

Ingredients

1 teaspoon olive oil
1 cup yellow onion, minced
2 garlic cloves, minced
4 cups organic low-sodium vegetable broth
1 tablespoon fresh parsley
1 tablespoon summer savory
1 whole bay leaf
2 cups yams, peeled and cubed
½ head of cabbage, chopped

Directions

Sauté onion and garlic in olive oil in a saucepan for 5 minutes, stirring occasionally. Pour in broth and add parsley, summer savory, and bay leaf. Bring to a boil, cover, and simmer for 20 minutes.

Gently place yams and cabbage into the soup and give it a little whirl, cover and simmer for another 20 minutes until the yam is fork-tender.

Vegan

Vegetarian

Gluten-Free

Dairy-Free

Paleo

Roasted Vegetable Soup

Yields 2 servings

Ingredients

3 medium carrots
1 yellow bell pepper
1 red bell pepper
2 teaspoons olive oil
⅛ teaspoon sea salt
¼ teaspoon coconut sugar
2 large tomatoes, halved
1 heaping tablespoon fresh parsley,
    chopped
1–2 garlic cloves, minced

2 tablespoons yellow onion, diced
1 teaspoon fresh basil, chopped
¼ teaspoon thyme
¼ teaspoon ground savory
1½–2 cups water
½ cup balsamic vinegar, plus 1 teaspoon
    balsamic vinegar
1 tablespoon maple syrup
Garnish with chopped chives and a few
    reserved roasted red peppers slivers

Directions

Chop carrots into 2-inch pieces, remove stem and seeds from bell peppers, and cut into slivers. Place carrot and bell peppers onto a baking sheet; coat with olive oil and sprinkle with sea salt and coconut sugar. Roast three rungs from top of oven at 500°F for 10 minutes; toss vegetables halfway through roast.

Remove roasting pan from the oven and roll tomato halves on the pan to coat with olive oil. Sprinkle parsley, garlic, onion, basil, thyme, and savory on top of all the vegetables. Place back into the oven and roast for another 10 minutes.

Continued on next page

Place all roasted vegetables into a pot, along with all the scrapings of herbs that remain on the roasting pan. You may opt to set aside a few roasted red pepper slivers as a garnish. Add water and 1 teaspoon balsamic vinegar; bring to a boil, reduce heat, cover, and simmer for 10 minutes.

In a separate small pot add ½ cup balsamic vinegar and maple syrup. Bring to a slow boil and cook for 5 minutes, stirring frequently, to create a balsamic reduction. Set aside.

Submerge a handheld mixer into your roasted vegetable soup pot and pulse a few times to purée. Add a bit more water for a lighter consistency.

Place a few ladles of soup into a serving bowl, top with a bit of roasted red peppers, drizzle a teaspoon of balsamic reduction on top, and a sprinkle of chives.

Vegan

Vegetarian

Gluten-Free

Dairy-Free

Taste of Tuscany

Yields 4 servings

Ingredients

1½ cups white beans, soaked overnight

6 cups water*

1 (2-inch) piece kombu

1 (6-inch) sprig fresh rosemary, oregano, and thyme

½ teaspoon dried marjoram

8-inch piece of cheesecloth or metal tea ball for fresh herbs

½ red onion

3 garlic cloves, minced

1 tablespoon Earth Balance Olive Oil Buttery Spread

1 red bell pepper, minced

4 large vine-ripened or heirloom tomatoes, cored

1 teaspoon 25 Star White Balsamic Vinegar

½ teaspoon sea salt

Garnish with any remaining herbs contained in ingredient list: finely chopped rosemary, oregano, thyme or marjoram (optional)

Directions

Rinse and remove debris from beans; soak in a large pot of water with kombu overnight.

Continued on next page

*Organic low-sodium vegetable broth or a mixture of half water and half vegetable broth can be substituted.

Place fresh rosemary, oregano, and thyme onto the center of cheesecloth and bring the edges together; tie to make an herb pouch. Set aside. Gathering fresh herbs and placing them into a metal tea ball also works well; just make sure the tea ball is securely closed before placing it into the bean pot.

Rinse beans and kombu after soaking, and place into a large pot with 6 cups fresh water. Bring to a boil, reduce heat to low, add the herb pouch, cover but leave lid slightly ajar for a creamier textured bean, and cook for approximately 1½ hours or until beans are soft.

While the beans are cooking, we'll prepare the good stuff. Place onion and garlic into a food processor; pulse until they are the size of rice grains; set aside in a bowl. Place bell pepper into a food processor; pulse until it is the size of rice grains; set aside in a separate bowl.

Place tomatoes into a food processor and pulse until the tomato is chopped but still contain chunks along with the liquid, yielding just over 2 cups; set aside.

Sauté onion and garlic in butter in a separate skillet for 10 minutes, tossing occasionally as they brown; add bell pepper and continue to sauté for an additional 5 minutes. Stir in tomatoes, sea salt and white balsamic. Cover and simmer approximately an hour while beans are cooking; stir occasionally.

When beans are tender, remove and discard herb pouch and kombu from the bean pot. Ladle a bit of the bean broth and reserve in a Mason jar for thinning the soup a little at a time. Leave just enough broth to cover the beans.

Stir in cooked tomatoes, bell pepper, onion, and garlic to the bean pot, adding a little broth at a time until you reach desired consistency. Cover and simmer 5 to 10 minutes to integrate the flavors. Ladle Taste of Tuscany into a serving bowl, top with fresh chopped herbs, if desired, and sea salt to taste.

Green Potato Soup

Yields 2–4 servings

Ingredients

⅓ cup Naked Almonds (see page 69)
½ cup coconut milk
1 tablespoon nutritional yeast
1 tablespoon olive oil
1 yellow onion, chopped
4 garlic cloves, minced
2 cups baby celery with leaves, chopped
4 cups organic low-sodium vegetable broth

3 cups white potatoes, chopped into
    1-inch squares
1 tablespoon marjoram
1 tablespoon fresh parsley
1 teaspoon sea salt
⅛ teaspoon crushed peppercorn
Garnish with fresh parsley sprigs and 1
    tablespoon lemon, juiced (optional)

Directions

Place Naked Almonds, nutritional yeast, and coconut milk in a high speed blender for approximately 45 seconds until creamy. Set almond base aside.

Sauté garlic and onion in olive oil in a large pot for 3 minutes. Add baby celery and sauté for an additional minute. Add broth, potatoes, marjoram, and 1 tablespoon parsley; bring to a boil, reduce heat, simmer, cover, and cook for 20 minutes.

Add sea salt, crushed peppercorn, and almond base. Stir, cover, and cook for an additional 15 minutes or until the potatoes are soft. Submerge a hand held mixer directly into the pot and pulse a few times until you reach desired consistency. Ladle into a serving bowl and garnish with fresh parsley sprigs and lemon juice.

Tomato Basil Gazpacho

Yields 2 servings

Ingredients

3 vine-ripened tomatoes, divided
2 inches English cucumber, diced
1 garlic, minced
½ red bell pepper, diced
½ green bell pepper, diced
1 tablespoon fresh basil, minced
1 tablespoon olive oil
2 tablespoons lemon juice
½ teaspoon sea salt
Dash pepper

Directions

Core 2 tomatoes and slice in half. Place the tomato seed-side against a hand held grater, and shred tomato over a bowl by sliding it back and forth until only the skin remains; discard tomato skins. Pour tomato liquid into a high speed blender and blend for 45 seconds until creamy. Set aside.

Core and dice 1 tomato; pour into a large bowl and add all remaining ingredients. Top with creamy tomato from the blender and stir. Divide and ladle into two small serving glasses and chill in the refrigerator for at least 1 hour.

Vegan   Vegetarian   Gluten-Free   Dairy-Free   Paleo

Rustic Sweet Pea & Potato Soup

Yields 2 servings

Ingredients

1 cup yellow onion, chopped
3 garlic cloves, minced
1 small carrot, diced
1 teaspoon olive oil
1 red bell pepper, diced, stem and seeds
    removed
1 tablespoon Earth Balance Olive Oil
    Buttery Spread
2 dark red heirloom tomatoes (approx. 2
    cups with juices), diced

1 bay leaf
1 teaspoon Adobo seasoning
1¾ cups water
1 teaspoon sea salt
½ cup peas
1 medium-sized Yukon Gold potato, cut
    into ½ inch-squares (yields approx.
    1–1 ½ cups)
¼ teaspoon sweet paprika

Directions

Combine onion, garlic, and carrot onto a baking sheet and drizzle with olive oil. Roast three rungs from the top of the oven at 500°F for 15 minutes, tossing once midway through roast. Set aside.

Sauté red bell pepper in butter in a large saucepan for 8 minutes. Add tomato, bay leaf, Adobo seasoning, and water. Bring to a boil, reduce heat, cover, and simmer for 45 minutes.

Ladle half of the tomato and bell pepper from the saucepan with a bit of juices, purée in a blender and place back into pot. Add sea salt, peas, potatoes, paprika, and roasted onion, carrot, and garlic. Bring to a boil, reduce heat to low, cover, and cook for approximately 30 to 35 minutes or until the potatoes are fork-tender. Ladle into serving bowls and enjoy piping hot.

Vegan

Vegetarian

Gluten-Free

Dairy-Free

Russian Borscht

Yields 4 servings

Recipe inspired by my sister-in-law Oxana Smith, with love straight from Russia.

Ingredients

6 cups water*
2 large red potatoes, peeled and diced
2 bay leaves
1 teaspoon sea salt, plus a sprinkle for
    sautéing
2 carrots, ends removed and cut into
    small matchsticks
2 beets, peeled and diced
2 garlic cloves, minced

1 yellow onion, diced
¼ cup olive oil
¼ teaspoon pepper
3 ripened tomatoes
1 head cabbage, cored and shredded
4 fresh dill sprigs
Garnish with a few dollops of Homemade
    Sour Cream and/or fresh minced green
    onion, parsley, and dill (see page 261)

Directions

In a large pot, combine water, potatoes, bay leaves, and sea salt; bring to a boil, cover, and reduce heat to a low boil while preparing the veggies.

Continued on next page

*Water can be replaced with vegetable or chicken broth for a more robust flavor.

Sauté carrots, beets, garlic, and onion with oil in a skillet for 7 minutes; sprinkle a pinch of sea salt and pepper to taste.

Core tomatoes and slice in half. Place the tomato seed-side against a hand held grater, and shred tomato over a bowl by sliding it back and forth until only the skin remains; discard tomato skins.

Toss shredded tomatoes into the skillet over the sautéed veggies and stir. Cook for approximately 2 to 3 minutes and slowly pour all sautéed veggies into the soup pot when potatoes are nearly fork-tender; reduce heat, cover, and simmer.

Gather shredded cabbage in your hands a little at a time and give them big hugs to soften them; add cabbage to the soup pot. Cover and continue to simmer until cabbage is cooked but slightly crunchy.

Give your Borscht a little taste here and there, adding more sea salt and pepper to taste, if necessary, and checking the desired doneness of cabbage and potatoes. Ladle into serving bowl and top with your desired garnish.

Vegan

Vegetarian

Gluten-Free

Dairy-Free

Paleo-opt

Ecuadorian Caramelized Onion, Sundried Tomato & Popcorn

Yields 2 servings

Ingredients
15 vine-ripened tomatoes
2 tablespoons sun-dried tomato paste by Amore All Natural
1 large elephant garlic clove, sliced
¼ yellow onion, chopped
1 large red bell pepper, diced, stem and seeds removed
1 tablespoon Earth Balance Olive Oil Buttery Spread
1 teaspoon sea salt
½ teaspoon fresh thyme leaves
½ teaspoon fresh marjoram leaves
Handful Buddha Bowl Himalayan Sweet & Salty Organic Popcorn*

Directions
Bring a large pot of water to a rolling boil while slicing a shallow X at the bottom of each tomato; gently lower each tomato into the boiling water.

Continued on next page

*LesserEvil Budda Bowl Organic Popcorn Himalayan Pink can be substituted with homemade organic popcorn popped with coconut oil and sea salt. Paleo option: omit popcorn

Cook until tomato skins start to wrinkle. Drain water and allow tomatoes to cool. Core and peel tomatoes over a bowl, reserving liquid and discarding core and tomato skins. Set aside.

Sauté garlic, onion, and red bell pepper in butter in a large pot for 15 minutes, tossing occasionally, until onions start to caramelize and garlic browns. Add tomatoes, sun-dried tomato paste, salt, thyme, and marjoram to the caramelized veggies and bring to a boil. Reduce heat, cover, and simmer 30 minutes.

Pour soup into a high speed blender and purée for 40 seconds or until creamy and pour it back into pot. Ladle into serving bowls and top with popcorn.

Vegan **Vegetarian** **Gluten-Free** **Dairy-Free**

Macrobiotic Healing Soup

Yields 2–4 servings

Kombu's amazing health benefits include essential trace minerals, vitamin B12, and vitamin D. Kombu detoxifies the body by binding to heavy metals, expelling toxins from the body, and protecting against gamma radiation. It aids in digestion, improves blood circulation, prevents constipation, and balances alkaline and acid in the body. Kombu helps prevent cancer by leveling the body's pH, aiding in a stronger nervous system and higher absorption of calcium.

Miso will help to reestablish your intestinal tract and create healthy micro-flora, creating improved digestion and a healthier pH within the digestive tract.

Ingredients

1 cup organic firm tofu
4 cups water*
1 (6-inch) piece EDEN Kombu Sea
  Vegetable
½–1-inch ginger, sliced
1 cup mushrooms, sliced or whole**
1 celery stalk, sliced

1 green onion, sliced
½ nori sheet, ripped
3–4 tablespoons chickpea miso paste
1 teaspoon umeboshi paste
Garnish with 2 teaspoons sesame seeds
  and pinch sea salt (optional)

Continued on next page

---

*Vegetable broth can be substituted or half water half vegetable broth.
**Choose your favorite mushrooms.

Directions

First we will prep the tofu by pouring out the water after opening the package and placing the tofu on top of a clean cloth. Drape another cloth or multiple layers of paper towels over the top and pad down a bit to soak up liquid. You may even opt to place a cutting board or plate over the top of the cloth and allow to sit while preparing the remaining soup. Make sure the tofu is dry before cutting into cubes; this will allow the tofu to reabsorb the liquid from the miso.

Bring water to a boil in a small saucepan, break kombu into pieces, and add to the water along with ginger, celery, green onion, mushrooms, nori pieces, and prepared tofu; cover and reduce heat to simmer for 20 minutes.

When vegetables are to your tenderness, add a few tablespoons of soup broth to a small bowl and add the umeboshi and miso paste, whisk thoroughly and add it back to the soup. Stir the soup gently and allow it to simmer for 1 minute; ladle into a serving bowl and garnish with a few sesame seeds and a pinch of sea salt, if desired.

IN THE GARDEN

Vegan   Vegetarian Dairy-Free

Greek Pizza

Yields 2 servings

Ingredients
1 cup organic unbleached flour, plus 1
    tablespoon for dusting
1 teaspoon fast-acting yeast
1 teaspoon sunflower lethicin (optional)
¼ teaspoon sea salt

1 tablespoon olive oil, plus ½ teaspoon
    for greasing
¼ cup warm water
½ cup arugula
1 tomato, diced
10–15 green or Kalamata olives

Directions
Sift flour, yeast, sunflower lethicin, and sea salt in a bowl. Stir slightly with a spoon while adding 1 tablespoon olive oil and warm water until the ingredients clump together. Sprinkle 1 tablespoon flour on a dry cutting board and roll the pizza dough into a ball with hands. Knead for 8 minutes.

With a rolling pin, flatten and roll the dough into a 6-inch round pizza pie. Coat a baking sheet with ½ teaspoon oil and gently lay flattened pizza pie on top of the oil. Slide the baking sheet into the center of the oven, turn on the oven light, close the oven door, and allow the crust to rise for approximately 15 minutes to 1 hour, depending how thick you want your crust.

Remove pizza pie from the oven and set aside. Preheat the oven to 425°F and place the pizza pie back into the oven for approximately 15 to 20 minutes, depending on the crispness you prefer. Place the pizza pie onto a cutting board, add arugula, tomato, and olives to the top and slice into fourths.

Vegan

Vegetarian

Gluten-Free

Dairy-Free

Paleo

Roasted Sugar Pie Pumpkin & Cauliflower

Yields 4 servings

Ingredients

1 head cauliflower
¼ cup coconut milk*
1 tablespoon cumin
2 teaspoons turmeric
1 tablespoon chili powder
¼ teaspoon sweet paprika
1 teaspoon sea salt
1 tablespoon fresh lime juice

1 small garlic clove, minced
1–2 Thai chili peppers, chopped
½ small Sugar Pie pumpkin
    (approx. 2 pounds)
2 teaspoons coconut oil for greasing
    (optional)
Handful arugula, chopped

Directions

Remove cauliflower florets and set aside. Pour coconut milk into a large bowl; whisk in cumin, turmeric, chili powder, paprika, salt, lime, garlic, and Thai chili. Slather cauliflower florets in the mixture; set aside. Slice a small pumpkin in half and quarters. Set aside. No need to peel or remove seeds until after roasting.

Grease baking sheet with coconut oil and layer cauliflower florets, drizzling extra scrapings of coconut milk and spices over the top. Place pumpkin slices on the baking sheet cut-side down. Roast at 400°F for approximately 40 to 45 minutes. Once cool, carefully peel pumpkin skin off and discard seeds. Chop pumpkin into large chunks and place into a serving dish along with cauliflower florets. Toss in chopped arugula.

*Organic full-fat coconut milk in the can for this recipe works best.

Vegan

Vegetarian

Gluten-Free

Dairy-Free

Smoked Chili

Yields 4 servings

Ingredients

2 cups red kidney beans
1 tablespoon olive oil
1 yellow onion, chopped
4 garlic cloves, minced
3 heirloom tomatoes, diced
½ teaspoon smoked paprika
½ teaspoon chipotle seasoning
1 teaspoon cumin
1 teaspoon Mediterranean seasoning
½ teaspoon celery seed powder
¼ teaspoon liquid smoke

2 tablespoons fresh parsley, chopped
2 teaspoons chili powder
1 teaspoon red chili flakes
1 (2-inch) piece kombu
1 bay leaf
1 teaspoon sea salt
4 cups water
Garnish with chopped green onion,
    red chili pepper, and fresh parsley
    (optional)

Directions

Rinse and remove debris from beans. Set aside. Sauté onion and garlic in oil in a large saucepan for approximately 10 minutes. Add all the remaining ingredients, bring to a boil, reduce heat, cover, and simmer for approximately 3 hours until beans are tender.

Ladle Smoked Chili into a serving bowl and top with your favorite garnish.

Mung Beans & Potatoes

Yields 4 servings

Ingredients

2 tablespoons Earth Balance Olive Oil Buttery Spread
½ teaspoon fresh ginger, grated
1 garlic clove, minced
¼ teaspoon mustard powder
Pinch cayenne
½ teaspoon cumin
1 teaspoon fenugreek seeds

2 cups mini Yukon Gold potatoes, peeled and chopped
6 cups water
2 cup mung beans, presoaked overnight
½ cup parsley, chopped, plus 1 sprig chopped for garnish
1½ cup carrot, shredded
1 red bell pepper, chopped

Directions

Melt butter in large saucepan and add ginger, garlic, mustard powder, cayenne, and cumin. Sauté for 3 minutes. Place fenugreek seeds into a tea ball and drape over the edge of the saucepan. Soak and rinse peeled and chopped potatoes to eliminate remaining starch, then add potatoes, water, and all other ingredients to the large saucepan. Bring to a boil. Reduce heat, cover, and simmer for 30 minutes or until potatoes are fork-tender and the beans are soft.

Remove fenugreek tea ball and discard. Ladle mung beans and potatoes into a serving bowl and garnish with fresh parsley and your favorite add-ins.

Fun Add-Ins: Pinch of sea salt and drizzle of coconut aminos

Vegan   Vegetarian   Dairy-Free

Fried Udon & Cabbage

Yields 2–4 servings

Ingredients
¼ package of udon noodles
1 garlic cloves, minced
2 tablespoons walnut oil
½ cup yellow onion, chopped
1 teaspoon paprika
½ teaspoon crushed red pepper flakes
2 cups green cabbage, chopped and core removed
1 teaspoon cracked pepper

Directions
Boil 1 quart of water in a large saucepan, add udon noodles. Reduce heat, simmer uncovered for 10 minutes, drain, rinse. Set aside.

While the udon noodles are cooking, sauté garlic in walnut oil in a cast-iron skillet for 2 minutes to brown, slowly adding onion, paprika, crushed red pepper flakes, cabbage, and pepper. Stir occasionally for 10 minutes until cabbage is tender. If cabbage is too dry during the sauté, add 1 to 2 tablespoons water. Stir udon noodles into sautéed cabbage and continue to cook for an additional 2 minutes.

Vegan   Vegetarian   Gluten-Free   Dairy-Free

Fancy Falafels

Yields 2–4 servings

Ingredients

½ cup organic dry chickpeas
1 (2-inch) piece kombu
4 cups water
½ small white onion
2 large garlic cloves
¼ teaspoon coriander seeds
⅓ cup fresh parsley
2 teaspoons cumin

½ teaspoon chipotle seasoning
2 teaspoons black flax seeds
½ teaspoon baking soda
¼ teaspoon sea salt
½ cup coconut oil for frying
Garnish with a dollop of Tzatziki Dipping
    Sauce (see page 255)*

Directions

Soak chickpeas and kombu in water for at least 12 hours and up to 24 hours. Change water at least once during soak time. Discard kombu, drain and rinse chickpeas. Set aside in bowl. Place coriander seeds into a sandwich bag and crush with a rolling pin, set aside.

In a food processor, pulse chickpeas, onion, garlic, crushed coriander seeds, parsley, cumin, chipotle, flax seeds, baking soda, and sea salt. Pulse the food processor 1 to 2 seconds at a time, blending until the mixture is slightly mealy and not mushy. You may need to stop the food processor occasionally to scrape down the sides.

Continued on next page

*Coconut Milk Yogurt can be substituted for those who have a strong dairy intolerance (see page 257).

Gather a heaping tablespoon of falafel mixture in your hand and give it a firm hug to form a ball, but not too tight. Do not squeeze out the liquid while forming falafel balls. Continue to form each falafel and place them onto parchment paper. Set aside.

Preheat coconut oil in a very small saucepan; it should be hot, but not too high. Test the coconut oil by drizzling 1 to 2 drops of water over the top. The sound of sizzles is a green light to gently ladle one falafel at a time into the saucepan. Do not overcrowd these fancy falafels. Cook until crispy and golden. Do not cook for more than 2½ minutes total. Use a slotted spoon to gently roll falafels midway through cooking.

Remove each falafel and place onto a paper towel to strain oils. Arrange on a serving bowl and drizzle with Tzatziki.

Potato Pizzaiola

Yields 2–4 servings

Ingredients

¼ cup olive oil, plus 1 tablespoon olive oil
1 small yellow onion
4 large garlic cloves
16 ripe Roma tomatoes
1 teaspoon oregano, plus ¼ teaspoon
  oregano
1 teaspoon basil, plus ¼ teaspoon basil

1 teaspoon sea salt, plus ¼ teaspoon
¼ teaspoon cayenne
2 tablespoons smoked paprika
4–6 small red potatoes
¼ teaspoon thyme
1 teaspoon fresh marjoram leaves
Handful fresh basil leaves

Directions

Chop onion and garlic in a food processor until the size of large grains of rice. Sauté garlic and onion in a cast iron skillet with ¼ cup olive oil for approximately 5 minutes or until browned.

Core and roughly chop tomatoes, place in a food processor and pulse until well chopped, but not puréed. Pour tomatoes over sautéed garlic and onion, and add 1 teaspoon oregano, 1 teaspoon basil, 1 teaspoon sea salt, and ¼ teaspoon cayenne. Bring to a boil over medium heat, reduce to simmer, cover, and cook for 45 minutes, stirring occasionally.

Continued on next page

Remove lid from sauce and submerge a handheld mixer into the sauce and blend to desired consistency. Simmer uncovered for an additional 45 minutes to an hour, stirring occasionally so the sauce will not burn to the skillet. This reduction will allow the sauce to thicken. Stir in smoked paprika at this time to bring your sauce to a whole new level of dark, rich, and robust.

While the sauce is in reduction, prep the potatoes. Peel and chop to your desired thickness, rinse and set aside in a bowl. Drizzle potatoes with 1 tablespoon olive oil, ¼ teaspoon sea salt, fresh marjoram leaves, ¼ teaspoon basil, ¼ teaspoon oregano, and ¼ teaspoon thyme. Mix thoroughly and place potatoes on a baking sheet. Bake at 420°F for approximately 30 minutes or until fork-tender. Toss the potatoes once or twice while cooking.

Carefully spoon potatoes into pizzaiola sauce, mixing sauce over potatoes, cover and continue to simmer for approximately 5 minutes. Top with fresh basil leaves and serve hot.

Vegan Vegetarian Gluten-Free Dairy-Free

Picnic Bean Salad

Yields 2–4 servings

Ingredients

1 cup black beans
4 cups water
¼ yellow onion, diced
2 small red baby bell peppers, diced
2 large garlic cloves, minced
1 tablespoon fresh parsley, minced
1 teaspoon sea salt
1 teaspoon Adobo seasoning
1 avocado, diced
4 full fresh dill sprigs, ripped
1 tablespoon fresh lime juice, plus more if desired

Directions

Rinse and remove debris from beans. Place water, beans, onion, bell pepper, garlic, parsley, Adobo seasoning, and sea salt into a crock pot. Cook on high for 4 hours or until beans are soft. I like to give 'em a little stir once or twice during cook time.

Layer avocado dices and dill sprigs on the bottom of a 9x9-inch serving dish, gently pour beans over the top and drizzle with lime juice. Give it a few gentle tosses with a large spoon. Amazingly delicious with extra lime juice, fresh dill, and pinch of sea salt.

Vegan   Vegetarian   Gluten-Free-opt   Dairy-Free   Paleo-opt

Garden Spaghetti

Yields 2–4 servings

Ingredients
7 very large tomatoes
½ yellow onion, chopped
5 garlic cloves, smashed
¼ cup olive oil
½ teaspoon sea salt
½ green Italian sweet frying pepper, chopped, stem and seeds removed
¼ teaspoon oregano, parsley, thyme, and basil
1 bay leaf
1 package De Boles Organic Whole Wheat Spaghetti Style Pasta (optional)*
Garnish with sliced cherry tomatoes and toasted pine nuts (optional)

Directions
Bring a large pot of water to a rolling boil while slicing a shallow X at the bottom of each tomato, and use a melon baller to remove the top core. Gently lower each tomato into the pot carefully with a ladle. Cook until tomato skins start to wrinkle. Drain and rinse tomatoes with cold water; allow them to cool a bit. Peel and discard tomato skins. Cut tomatoes into fourths and set aside in a large bowl with all the tomato drippings.

Continued on next page

---

*Gluten-free and paleo option: spiralized and slightly steamed zucchini

Sauté garlic, onion, and Italian sweet pepper in olive oil in a large saucepan for 10 minutes, tossing occasionally. Add sea salt and herbs; stir for 1 minute. Pour in tomatoes with all the drippings, oregano, parsley, thyme, basil, and bay leaf. Bring to a boil, then reduce heat, cover, and simmer 1 hour.

Uncover, remove bay leaf, submerge a handheld mixer, and blend to desired consistency. Turn up heat to a low boil and cook uncovered for 1½ to 2 hours for the sauce to reduce and thicken.

Boil four quarts of water in a separate saucepan, add De Boles Organic Spaghetti, and cook for 6 to 8 minutes until al dente. Drain and rinse.

Ladle a cup of spaghetti into a serving dish and top with piping hot spaghetti sauce. Garnish with sliced cherry tomatoes and toasted pine nuts.

Vegan   Vegetarian   Gluten-Free   Dairy-Free   Paleo

Pizza Bowl

Yields 1–2 servings

Ingredients
2 tablespoons walnut oil
2 garlic cloves, minced
¼ cup yellow onion, chopped
½ red bell pepper, sliced
½ green bell pepper, sliced
1 cup crimini mushrooms, sliced
1 tablespoon parsley
2 tablespoons white balsamic vinegar
1 large dark red heirloom tomato, sliced with juices (yields approx. 2 cups)
2 cups spinach, chopped
2 tablespoons chives
Pinch sea salt and crushed red pepper flakes
Garnish with a drizzle coconut aminos (optional)

Directions
Sauté garlic, onion, and bell peppers in walnut oil for approximately 3 minutes. Add mushrooms, parsley, and balsamic vinegar; cook until vegetables are slightly tender, 2 to 3 minutes. Add sliced tomato with juices, spinach, and half of the chives; cook for 2 to 3 minutes and pour into a bowl. Top with remaining chives, sea salt, pepper flakes, and a drizzle of coconut aminos.

Vegan

Vegetarian

Gluten-Free

Dairy-Free

Smokey Texas Taters

Yields 4 servings

Ingredients

4 red potatoes
1 tablespoon peanut oil
½ teaspoon sea salt
¼ teaspoon basil
¼ teaspoon oregano
¼ teaspoon thyme

½ teaspoon smoked paprika
2 teaspoons fresh rosemary leaves, chopped
2 teaspoons fresh marjoram leaves, chopped

Directions

Peel and chop potatoes into steak fry wedges. Place in a bowl of cold water and soak for at least 5 minutes to remove some of the surface starch while gathering and preparing the herbs.

Set fresh chopped rosemary and marjoram aside to use at a later time. Whisk peanut oil, salt, basil, oregano, thyme, and smoked paprika in a separate bowl. Strain and rinse potatoes; pat dry a bit to remove excess water. Pour the oil and herb mixture over the potatoes; mix thoroughly and place potatoes on a baking sheet. Cook in a preheated oven at 420°F for approximately 20 to 30 minutes. Cook time may vary depending on the thickness of your potato wedges. Halfway through cook time, toss taters and sprinkle with fresh rosemary and marjoram. Devour à la carte or with Tzatziki Dipping Sauce (255). The crazy combo of heat from the Smokey Texas Taters dipped in the coolness of the Tzatziki is absolutely fabulous!

*Coconut Milk Yogurt can be substituted for those who have a strong dairy intolerance (257).

UNDER THE SEA

Gluten-Free-opt Dairy-Free

Steamed Mussels in Tomato Tzatziki Sauce

Yields 4 servings

Ingredients

½ yellow onion, minced
3 garlic cloves, minced
1 red bell pepper, diced
1 tablespoon Earth Balance Olive Oil Buttery Spread
1 tablespoon fresh parsley, chopped
1 tablespoon fresh basil, chopped
½ teaspoon celery seed powder
6 vine-ripened tomatoes, chopped, liquid reserved

1 teaspoon white balsamic vinegar
1 teaspoon sweet paprika
1 bay leaf
½ teaspoon Tzatziki seasoning
½ cup mushrooms, chopped
¼ teaspoon sea salt
⅛ teaspoon pepper
2 pounds mussels
1 package De Boles Organic Whole Wheat Spaghetti Style Pasta (optional)*

Directions

Sauté onion, garlic, and bell pepper in butter for 15 minutes in a cast-iron skillet. Add all other ingredients except mussels and spaghetti. Bring to boil, reduce heat, cover, and simmer for 2 hours.

Continued on next page

---

*Gluten-free option: vegetable pasta or omit pasta altogether and enjoy Steamed Mussels in Tomato Tzatziki Sauce à la carte.

Allow to slightly cool, and place sauce into a high speed blender. Blend for approximately 20 seconds and pour back into the skillet. Return to a boil, reduce heat, and simmer while preparing mussels and spaghetti.

Wash mussels and place into tomato tzatziki sauce, cover, and cook for five minutes or until all the mussels have popped open. Remove the opened mussels and set aside so that they do not overcook. Discard any mussels that have not opened. Pour all steamed mussels back into the tomato tzatziki sauce, remove from heat, give those little puppies a toss, and serve over spaghetti or enjoy à la carte.

To make De Boles Organic Spaghetti, boil four quarts of water in a large pot, add noodles, and cook for 6 to 8 minutes until al dente. Drain and rinse.

Ladle a portion of spaghetti onto a serving dish and top with Steamed Mussels in Tomato Tzatziki Sauce.

Pasta with Mediterranean Mussels

Yields 2–4 servings

Ingredients

½ red onion, chopped fine
2 garlic cloves, minced
2 tablespoon Earth Balance Olive Oil
    Buttery Spread
4 vine-ripened tomatoes, chopped, liquid
    reserved
2 tablespoons fresh parsley, chopped
½ teaspoon celery seed powder
¼ teaspoon crushed red pepper flakes
¼ teaspoon white balsamic vinegar
¼ teaspoon cumin
1 tablespoon fresh basil, chopped
¼ teaspoon Adobo seasoning

1 bay leaf
¼ teaspoon sea salt
½ pound mussels
1 package De Boles Organic Whole
    Wheat Spaghetti Style Pasta*

Directions

Sauté garlic and onion in butter in a cast-iron skillet for 10 minutes; stir occasionally until onions caramelize. Add all other ingredients except mussels and spaghetti, cover, and simmer for 45 minutes. Stir occasionally.

Continued on next page

---

*Gluten-free option: vegetable pasta or spiralized and slightly steamed zucchini.

Wash mussels and place into the sauce. Cover and cook for 5 minutes or until all the mussels have popped open. Remove the opened mussels and set aside so that they do not overcook. Discard any mussels that have not opened. Remove the meat from each mussel and place back into the Mediterranean sauce, give those little puppies a toss, and remove from heat.

Boil four quarts of water in a separate saucepan, add De Boles Organic Spaghetti and cook for 6 to 8 minutes until al dente. Drain and rinse. Pour into Mediterranean sauce and toss gently before serving.

Grilled Pineapple Salmon

Yields 2 servings

Ingredients

⅓ cup fresh pineapple juice
¼ teaspoon garlic powder
1 teaspoon honey
¼ teaspoon ginger powder
2 (1-inch) salmon fillets
⅓ cup walnut oil*

Directions

Whisk garlic powder, honey, ginger, and pineapple juice in a small bowl. Pour over salmon fillets and marinate overnight in the refrigerator for at least 1 hour; reserve marinade for basting.

Preheat barbecue grill at 450°F; a very hot grill works best. Coat walnut oil liberally on the grill with a long handled barbecue brush.

Place salmon on the grill, skin-side up, cover, and cook for 2 minutes. Gently turn salmon over with a large spatula, baste with remaining marinade, cover, and cook for 5 minutes only. Remove from heat and serve hot off the grill.

---

*Substitute oils: macadamia, coconut, or olive oil

Gluten-Free   Dairy-Free   Paleo

Tex-Mex Shrimp on the Barbie

Yields 2–4 servings

Ingredients
¼ cup olive oil
⅛ teaspoon sea salt
1 teaspoon fresh lime juice
1 teaspoon garlic, minced
⅛ teaspoon chipotle seasoning
$\frac{1}{16}$ teaspoon crushed peppercorn
1 pound uncooked deveined shrimp, tails on

Directions
Whisk olive oil, sea salt, lime juice, garlic, chipotle, and crushed peppercorn in a small bowl. Pour over washed and deveined shrimp and marinate in the refrigerator for at least 1 hour; reserve marinade for basting.

Preheat barbecue grill to 400°F. Place each shrimp on a metal skewer and place on the grill. Cover and cook for 2 to 3 minutes. Gently turn shrimp over with a large spatula. Cover and cook for 2 to 3 minutes. Shrimp is done when it turns orange. Remove from heat and serve hot off the grill with a squeeze of lime juice. Top over your favorite mixed greens.

Jambalaya

Yields 4 servings

Ingredients

3 cups uncooked peeled and deveined shrimp*

2 cups uncooked scallops

½ onion, diced

3 garlic cloves, chopped

1 orange bell pepper, diced

1 red Anaheim pepper, diced

1 tablespoon olive oil

1 all natural chicken sausage link, chopped, by Aidell's (optional)

1½ cups organic low-sodium vegetable broth

3 cups heirloom tomatoes, diced, liquid reserved

1 teaspoon thyme

½ teaspoon basil

⅛ teaspoon ground peppercorn

¼ teaspoon red pepper flakes

1 bay leaf

2 jalapeno pepper slices (optional)

Garnish with fresh chopped basil, green onion, diced tomatoes, and a squeeze of lime juice (optional)

Directions

Rinse shrimp and scallops in cool water and pat dry; set aside. If using frozen seafood, place shrimp and scallops in a fine mesh strainer over a bowl and cover with cold water. Allow to soak for 10 minutes, lift strainer out of water, pour water out, and refill with fresh cold water; allow to soak an additional 10 minutes or until defrosted. Lift strainer, place shrimp and scallops on a paper towel, and pat dry.

---

*Shrimp can be cooked shells-on; it yields a rich flavor. Just be sure to bring plenty of napkins to the table. It's going to get messy; how fun!

Sauté onion, garlic, and Anaheim peppers in olive oil in a large cast-iron skillet for approximately 2 minutes, stirring occasionally.

Add broth, sausage, tomatoes, any juices from the diced tomatoes, bay leaf, thyme, basil, peppercorn, red pepper flakes, and jalapeno slices for a hot and spicy Jambalaya. Bring to a boil, reduce heat, cover, and simmer for 10 minutes.

Add shrimp and scallops, bring to a boil, cover, and simmer for an additional 5 to 6 minutes until shrimp turns orange and scallops are opaque.

Ladle into serving bowl and enjoy as a stand-alone soup or serve atop steamed Organic Jasmine Rice* by Lotus Foods. The juices from the Jambalaya will soak into the rice and make it amazingly delicious and satisfying.

---

*Paleo option: omit rice

Hawaiian Furikake Salmon

Yields 2 servings

Ingredients

1½ tablespoons Furikake Seasoning
  (see page 273)
3 tablespoons Soy-Free Vegenaise
  (optional)*
½ cup coconut aminos

1 tablespoon honey
1 tablespoon red miso
1½ pounds wild-caught salmon, no more
  than ⅝-inch thick
Garnish with fresh cilantro (optional)

Directions

Whisk 1½ tablespoons Furikake Seasoning with 3 tablespoons Soy-Free Vegenaise to create the creamy Furikake Seasoning mix; set aside.

Whisk coconut aminos, honey, and red miso until creamy to create miso sauce. Pour into the bottom of a shallow oven-safe casserole dish.

Wash salmon and pat dry; slather the top with creamy Furikake Seasoning mix and place salmon skin-side down on top of miso sauce. Cover with foil and bake at 350°F for 15 minutes. Remove the foil and broil for 3 to 5 minutes. The salmon is done when it flakes off easily with a fork. Remove from oven and garnish with cilantro.

---

*Vegenaise can be substituted with Earth Balance Olive Oil Buttery Spread or just use Furikake Seasoning alone. It all depends on if you're in the mood for creamy, buttery, or sticking to the lighter side. Either way, this salmon will be amazing.

Gluten-Free Dairy-Free Paleo

Thai Shrimp Soup

Yields 2–4 servings

Ingredients

1 teaspoon coconut oil
2 garlic cloves, minced
½ teaspoon ginger, grated
½ cup yellow onion, minced
2 cups organic low-sodium vegetable
   broth
½ teaspoon lemon peel, grated
1 teaspoon crushed red pepper flakes
½ red bell pepper, sliced

1 cup mushrooms, halved
1 cup coconut milk
1 tablespoon red curry paste
1 tablespoon green curry paste (optional)
1 pound uncooked peeled and deveined
   shrimp
Garnish with fresh chopped cilantro and
   lime juice (optional)

Directions

Sauté garlic, onion, and ginger in coconut oil in a cast-iron skillet for 2 minutes. Add vegetable broth, lemon peel, red pepper flakes, bell pepper, and mushrooms. Bring to a boil, then reduce heat, cover, and simmer for 10 minutes.

Stir in coconut milk and curry paste; stir until dissolved. Add shrimp, bring to a boil, then reduce heat, and simmer 5 to 6 minutes until shrimp turns orange. Ladle into serving bowl and garnish with fresh cilantro and lime juice. Enjoy as a stand-alone soup or serve with steamed Organic Jasmine Rice* by Lotus Foods.

---

*Paleo option: omit rice

Shrimp Spring Rolls

Yields 4 servings

Ingredients

8 wild-caught jumbo shrimp, pre-frozen
   with tails
2 tablespoons olive oil
6 ounces thin rice noodles, straight cut
½ carrot
¼ red bell pepper

8 round rice paper sheets
8 small lettuce leaves
3 mint sprigs with leaves
8 cilantro sprigs with leaves
Thai Peanut Sauce, for dipping
   (see page 259)

Directions

Defrost shrimp in a fine mesh strainer over a bowl and cover with cold water. Allow to soak for 10 minutes, then lift strainer out of water, pour water out, and refill with fresh cold water. Allow to soak an additional 10 minutes or until defrosted. Lift strainer, place shrimp on a paper towel, and pat dry.

Sauté shrimp in oil over medium heat for 1 minute per side until they turn orange; set aside to cool. Peel and devein cooled shrimp, slice in half lengthwise and remove membrane. Rinse and set aside.

Bring a saucepan full of water to a boil. Pour in rice noodles and turn down heat to a low boil. Cook for 5 minutes, stirring occasionally. Drain and rinse noodles under cool water, and set aside in a strainer.

Continued on next page

Cut carrot and bell pepper lengthwise into finger-sized strips, and remove mint and cilantro leaves from sprigs. Set all vegetables and herbs aside.

Fill a very wide skillet with ½-inch water and heat until it just starts to boil. Remove from the stove and place the skillet on an oven mitt next to all the other ingredients used to make spring rolls: lettuce, shrimp, rice noodles, carrot, bell pepper, and herbs.

Now for the important part; make sure you have a large, dry, clean surface to work with, preferably a large cutting board that you can wipe clean after making each roll. Take 1 sheet of rice paper and hold one side, gently dip it into the warm water in the skillet for 1 to 2 seconds only. Pull the rice paper out of the water and allow the water to run off.

Turn the rice paper in your hands and dip the remaining dry sides for 1 to 2 seconds and allow the water to run off. Do not oversoak the rice paper or it will become soggy and difficult to use.

Place the pre-moistened rice paper sheet onto the dry surface, preferably a cutting board. Place 1 lettuce leaf across the outermost center of the round—be sure to leave 1 inch at the base of the round free of produce for folding—and line a few vegetable strips on top of the lettuce. Layer a pinch of rice noodles next to the vegetables, then layer 2 shrimp slices, and a couple mint and cilantro leaves in a row along the rice paper.

Now that you have your rice paper round arranged, grab the end of the rice paper near the lettuce end and start to create two small rolls; turn in the free end of the rice paper to close it up, and continue to roll until it is sealed. Set aside and continue rolling all the desired spring rolls. When completed, slice each roll in half and arrange on a serving platter; dip into Thai Peanut Sauce. Any uneaten spring rolls can be rolled individually with plastic wrap and stored in the refrigerator for 1 day only.

Crab Spring Rolls

Yields 4 servings

Ingredients

1 ounce Alaskan king crab legs
6 ounces thin rice noodles; straight cut
½ cucumber
Three mint sprigs with leaves
Handful sprouts
8 round rice paper sheets

8 small lettuce leaves
A few fresh chives or thin tips of green onion
1 teaspoon black sesame seeds (optional)
Thai Peanut Sauce, for dipping (see page 259)
Garnish with fresh lime wedges

Directions

Steam crab legs for 3 minutes; set aside and allow to cool. Over-steaming will shrink the crab meat and make it tough. Crack shells and scoop out crab meat; shred and set aside in a bowl.

Bring a saucepan full of water to a boil. Pour in rice noodles and turn down heat to a low boil; cook for 5 minutes, stirring occasionally. Drain and rinse noodles under cool water, and set aside in a strainer.

Cut cucumber lengthwise into finger-sized strips, and remove mint leaves from sprigs; set cucumber and mint leaves aside.

Fill a very wide skillet with ½-inch water and heat until it just starts to boil. Remove from the stove and place the skillet on an oven mitt next to all the other ingredients used to make spring rolls: lettuce, crab meat, rice noodles, cucumber, sprouts, mint leaves, chives, and sesame seeds.

Continued on next page

Now for the important part: make sure you have a large, dry, clean surface to work with, preferably a large cutting board that you can wipe clean after making each roll. Take 1 sheet of rice paper and hold one side, gently dip it into the warm water in the skillet for 1 to 2 seconds only. Pull the rice paper out of the water and allow the water to run off.

Turn the rice paper in your hands and dip the remaining dry sides for 1 to 2 seconds and allow the water to run off. Do not oversoak the rice paper or it will become soggy and difficult to use.

Place the pre-moistened rice paper sheet onto the dry surface, preferably a cutting board, place 1 lettuce leaf across the outermost center of the round and be sure to leave 1 inch at the base of the round free of produce for folding. Line a few cucumber strips on the top of lettuce, layer a pinch of sprout, a pinch of rice noodles, a bit of crab meat, and a couple mint leaves in a row along the rice paper.

Now that you have your rice paper round arranged, grab the end of the rice paper near the lettuce end and start to create two small rolls. Turn in the free end to close it up and continue to roll until almost to the end; add a pinch of sesame seeds and chives draping out of the folded end, and continue rolling all the desired spring rolls. When completed, slice each roll in half and arrange onto a serving platter; dip into Thai Peanut Sauce.

Any uneaten spring rolls can be rolled individually with plastic wrap and stored in the refrigerator for 1 day only.

LION'S DEN

Savory Beef Stew

Yields 4 servings

Ingredients

2 pounds Angus beef for stew, cut into 1-inch squares
4 tablespoons fresh garlic, minced
4 teaspoons summer savory
½ teaspoon cayenne pepper
2 tablespoons olive oil
4 green onions, chopped
4 cups crimini mushrooms, chopped

2–3 cups carrots, chopped
4 tablespoons fresh parsley, chopped
2 cups water
1 whole Anaheim pepper, stem and seeds removed
1 bay leaf
1 teaspoon sea salt
1 tablespoon ground savory

Directions

Combine beef, garlic, summer savory, and cayenne into a bowl and mix thoroughly. Preheat cast-iron skillet and add olive oil and the beef mixture. Cook for 2 minutes, stirring occasionally to brown the beef and infuse the flavors.

Add green onion, mushroom, carrot, and parsley; cook for 2 minutes. You may need to cook the beef and vegetables into 2 separate batches since it is a large quantity.

Add water, whole Anaheim pepper, and bay leaf to slow cooker and turn on high. Add all ingredients from the cast-iron skillet, beef, and vegetables, making sure to scrape all the herbs and drippings into the slow cooker. Sprinkle in sea salt and ground savory, cover, and cook on high for 2 hours; then turn heat to low for an additional 2½ hours or until beef is tender.

Herbed Filet Mignon & Lemon Butter Dressing

Yields 2 servings

Inspired by Bebe Savage, my daughter, a new creative chef in the making.

Ingredients for filets
2 filet mignons 1¾-inch thick
1 teaspoon sea salt

Ingredients for rub
4 teaspoons Earth Balance Olive Oil
   Buttery Spread, melted
½ teaspoon onion powder
Dash sea salt and cayenne
2 teaspoons fresh lemon juice
2 teaspoons water

½ teaspoon chipotle seasoning
2 teaspoons chives, chopped
2 teaspoons garlic powder
½ teaspoon dried sweet basil
½ teaspoon ground mustard
½ teaspoon caper liquid by La Pedriza

Directions for filets
Season each side of filets heavily with sea salt, set aside for 30 minutes; this allows moisture to be drawn from filets.

Continued on next page

Directions to cook filets

Preheat a griddle or small nonstick skillet over medium heat at approximately 400°F. Gently place filets on the hot griddle and cook for 9 minutes.

Turn the filets over just once and cook for 9 minutes. Rotate each filet on its sides to brown the edges for a few seconds. The filets are now medium rare and tender.

Remove from heat immediately and transfer filets onto a serving dish; drizzle a bit of lemon butter dressing onto each filet. Best served with Roasted Herb'd Tomatoes (211) or other vegetable sides.

Directions for rub

Whisk all rub ingredients thoroughly and pat seasoning onto filets. Allow the rub to marinate while making the lemon butter dressing.

Directions for lemon butter dressing

Whisk all lemon butter ingredients and set aside. This is to be used after filets are cooked as a garnish.

Ingredients for lemon butter dressing

2 tablespoons Earth Balance Olive Oil Buttery Spread, melted
2 teaspoons chives, finely chopped
Dash salt, pepper, thyme, and smoked paprika
2 tablespoons fresh lemon juice.

Curry Chicken & Coconut Jasmine

Yields 2–4 servings

Ingredients

4–6 skinless chicken thighs*
2–3 tablespoons curry powder
2 tablespoons sweet paprika
1 teaspoon sea salt
1 teaspoon cracked pepper
1 teaspoon ginger powder
½ teaspoon cayenne
½ yellow onion, chopped
6 garlic cloves, smashed

1 tablespoon coconut oil
2 carrots, grated
1½–2 cups coconut milk
Serve with Coconut Jasmine Rice
    (see page 220)
Garnish with your favorites toppings;
    chopped fresh cilantro, mint, basil,
    drizzle of Greek Gods Plain Kefir
    (optional)**

Directions

Wash chicken, cut into pieces, and set aside. Combine curry, paprika, sea salt, pepper, ginger, and cayenne into a small bowl and whisk with a fork. Dry toast seasoning in a nonstick skillet over low/medium heat for 1 minute, stirring continuously to bring out flavors; set aside.

Continued on next page

---

*Chicken breast can be substituted; reduce cook time.
**Coconut Milk Yogurt can be substituted for those who have a strong dairy intolerance (see page 257).

Sauté onion and garlic in coconut oil in a separate skillet for 5 minutes, stirring occasionally. Carefully add chicken pieces over sauté and brown each side for 1 minute.

Pour coconut milk into slow cooker and gently pour in your sauté of chicken, onion, and garlic, making sure to scape skillet for drippings. Sprinkle the dry toasted seasoning and shredded carrots over the top.

Cover and cook on low for approximately 1 hour. Give it a little stir and cook for an additional hour or so until the chicken is fork-tender; serve with Coconut Jasmine Rice.

Author's note: I like to get a big wide bowl and place chicken in the center, drizzle sauce over the top, and add chopped fresh herbs, along with a few tablespoons of milk kefir. Not only is it good for you, but it makes everything rich and creamy and so darn delicious.

Margo's Armenian Dolma

Yields 4–6 servings

Recipe inspired by my friend Adelina Nazaryan from Los Angeles.

Ingredients

6 zucchini

1 cup raw grass fed ground beef (optional)*

1 cup raw rice by Lotus Foods**

1 tablespoon Red Pepper Paste (see page 269)

1 large garlic clove, minced, plus 2 large garlic cloves for tomato sauce

½ cup yellow onion, minced

1 tablespoon fresh parsley, chopped

⅛ cup fresh basil, minced

⅛ cup fresh cilantro, minced

¼ teaspoon celery seed

½ teaspoon sea salt, plus ½ teaspoon sea salt for tomato sauce

¼ teaspoon pepper

6 tomatoes, cored and halved

Directions

Rinse rice thoroughly and place in a bowl of hot water to soak while preparing the dolma mix. Cut the tops of zucchini and scoop out the center with a spoon or melon ball scoop. Discard all seeds and pulp, except ½ cup pulp. Chop the ½ cup zucchini pulp into the size of rice grains and place in a large mixing bowl. Drain rice and add

Continued on next page

*Beef can be substituted with ground lamb or turkey. Vegan option: replace meat with more rice and a variety of veggies.

to chopped zucchini pulp. Mix in beef, red pepper paste, 1 large minced garlic clove, onion, parsley, basil, cilantro, celery seed, ½ teaspoon sea salt, and pepper. Mix thoroughly with hands and stuff zucchini, packing mixture down and filling to the top. Set rounds aside.

Blend ½ teaspoon sea salt, 2 large garlic cloves, and tomatoes in a high speed blender until liquefied. Pour tomato liquid into a saucepan and bring to a boil; reduce heat to medium and cook uncovered for 30 to 45 minutes. This reduction will evaporate the liquid, leaving a tomato sauce.

Fill a large pot with approximately ¼ inches water and gently arrange filled zucchini into the pot so they are hugging each other snuggly. If they are not snug, they may fall apart while cooking. The water should be approximately ¼ the way up the sides of the zucchini. Spoon some tomato sauce on top of each round and pour a bit of sauce into the pot so that the liquid is not more than halfway up the sides of the zucchini; reserve remaining sauce for serving.

Bring zucchini with liquid to a boil, then reduce heat to low, cover, and cook for approximately 3 hours or until the zucchini have become tender. Use large tongs to remove rounds very gently onto a serving dish. Ladle some tomato sauce from the zucchini pot or from the reserved tomato sauce around Margo's Armenian Dolma and enjoy. Traditionally eaten with yogurt blended with crushed garlic.

Leftover dolma can be stored in the refrigerator for up to 3 days and may be reheated in the oven or small toaster oven.

**Paleo option; omit rice and add more meat and veggies.

Gluten-Free

Dairy-Free

Paleo

Grilled Savory Lamb Chops

Yields 4 servings

Ingredients

1 teaspoon fresh rosemary, chopped
1 small garlic clove, chopped
¼ teaspoon thyme leaves
½ teaspoon ground savory
¼ teaspoon sea salt
⅛ teaspoon peppercorn
2 tablespoons olive oil
4 small lamb chops

Directions

Whisk rosemary, garlic, thyme, savory, sea salt, peppercorn, and oil in small bowl. Place lamb chops in marinade and coat thoroughly; refrigerate overnight or at least 4 hours.

Remove chops from refrigerator and allow to come down to room temperature, approximately 20 minutes. Preheat barbecue grill to 400°F and place each chop on the grill; cook for approximately 3 to 5 minutes. Turn the chops over with barbeque tongs and cook 3 to 5 minutes, depending upon thickness and preferred wellness. Remove from grill and serve with fresh arugula.

Grilled Rosemary Chicken

Yields 3–4 servings

Ingredients

1 teaspoon fresh garlic, minced
3 tablespoons walnut oil
2 teaspoons fresh rosemary, chopped
1 tablespoon Dijon mustard
1½ tablespoons lemon juice

Pinch ground peppercorn
Pinch sea salt
3 chicken breasts
Garnish with fresh rosemary and
    peppercorn

Directions

Whisk garlic, oil, rosemary, Dijon, lemon juice, peppercorn, and sea salt in a bowl; set marinade aside. Use a sharp knife to make a few holes in the chicken breasts and place in marinade. Cover and refrigerate overnight.

Preheat barbecue grill to 400°F, then place chicken on grill and close the lid; grill for 5 minutes. Open the lid and flip the chicken over; close the lid and grill for 5 to 7 minutes, depending upon the thickness of your chicken. Do not open the lid during cooking times. Place the thickest chicken breast on a cutting board and slice through the middle. It should be white and juicy when done.

Remove chicken from grill and garnish with fresh rosemary and peppercorn. Pairs well with Roasted Roots & Fresh Herbs (215) or Zucchini Sauté (209).

Grilled Chicken Teriyaki

Yields 2–4 servings

Ingredients
1 pound boneless skinless chicken thighs
1 teaspoon honey
¼ cup coconut aminos
1 teaspoon sesame oil
¼ teaspoon onion powder
⅛ teaspoon ginger powder

Directions
Wash chicken and set aside in a glass bowl. Whisk honey, coconut aminos, sesame oil, onion powder, and ginger powder in a small saucepan and bring to a boil; reduce heat to a low boil for 5 minutes.

Pour teriyaki sauce over chicken and coat well; cover and marinate overnight in the refrigerator.

Preheat barbecue grill to 350°F, then place chicken pieces on grill; close the lid and cook for 7 minutes. Open the lid, turn the chicken pieces over with barbeque tongs; close the lid and cook 7 minutes or until done. Do not lift the lid during cooking time. Pairs well with shredded cabbage and Furikake String Beans (225).

Gluten-Free

Dairy-Free

Paleo

Grilled Moroccan Lamb Chops

Yields 4 servings

Ingredients
3 mint leaves
1 small garlic clove, minced
½ teaspoon paprika
1 teaspoon cumin
½ teaspoon sea salt
¼ cup olive oil
Pinch cayenne pepper
4 small lamb chops

Directions
Roll mint leaves in between your fingers, then chop finely. Whisk chopped mint leaves, garlic, paprika, cumin, sea salt, oil, and cayenne in a small bowl. Place lamb chops in marinade and coat thoroughly; refrigerate overnight or at least 4 hours.

Remove chops from refrigerator and allow to come down to room temperature, approximately 20 minutes. Preheat barbecue grill to 400°F and place each chop on the grill; cook for approximately 3 to 5 minutes. Turn the chops over with barbeque tongs and cook 3 to 5 minutes, depending upon thickness and preferred wellness. Remove from grill and serve with fresh arugula.

Irish Brisket & Cabbage

Yields 6+ servings

Ingredients

4 pounds brisket with pickling spice included
1 cup organic low-sodium vegetable broth
½ cup water
2 bay leaves
1 teaspoon mustard powder
1 large garlic clove, mashed
1 cup yellow onion, chopped
1 teaspoon caraway seeds
¼ teaspoon smoked paprika
Dash cayenne
4 whole carrots, ends removed, peeled and halved
1 head cabbage, quartered
8–10 small red potatoes, chopped
Garnish with fresh parsley (optional)

Directions

Rinse brisket and place into a slow cooker. Top with vegetable broth, water, and all other ingredients. Cover and cook on high for 4 to 5 hours or on low for 7 to 8 hours until corned beef is fork-tender.

Remove corned beef, slice, and serve with vegetables and potatoes; sprinkle with fresh chopped parsley and drizzle with a bit of cooking juices.

Smoked Apple Pulled Pork Tostadas

Yields 6+ servings

Ingredients

4–5 pounds pork butt
1 cup fresh apple juice*
1 teaspoon sea salt
4 garlic cloves, smashed
1 tablespoon Bragg Liquid Aminos
1 tablespoon hickory liquid smoke
2 tablespoons maple syrup
½ teaspoon smoked paprika

½ teaspoon chili powder
½ teaspoon mustard powder
1 package organic corn tortillas
1 tablespoon olive oil for frying
1 avocado, diced
1 lime, cut into wedges
Garnish with crumbled feta and cilantro

Directions

Rinse pork butt and trim excess fat, and place in a slow cooker. Pour apple juice over the top and add sea salt, garlic, liquid aminos, liquid smoke, maple syrup, paprika, chili powder, and mustard powder. Cook on low for 5 to 6 hours or until fork-tender.

Fry organic corn tortillas in a cast iron skillet with olive oil over medium high heat until crisp; approximately 1 minute on each side. Remove from heat and blot oil with a paper towel.

Use two forks to gently pull the pork into shreds while it's still in the slow cooker. Use tongs to gather a bit of pulled pork; allow juices to drain a bit and top crispy corn tortillas. Add a sprinkle of feta, avocado, cilantro and a squeeze from a lime wedge.

---

*Fresh juiced apples are preferred, but if you are purchasing apple juice, choose a brand that does not contain ingredients that list: concentrate, citric acid, high fructose corn syrup, added sugar, or preservatives. Read labels carefully; Gee Whiz is a great brand!

Gluten-Free

Dairy-Free

Paleo

Cast-Iron Grilled Fried Steak

Yields 2–4 servings

Ingredients
1 pound flank steak, 1-inch thick*
2 teaspoons Organic Rib Eye Steak Seasoning by Spicely Organics
½ teaspoon sea salt
1 teaspoon Earth Balance Olive Oil Buttery Spread for frying (optional)

Directions
Generously sprinkle both sides of steak with sea salt, pat down with fingertips, and set aside for 40 minutes on the countertop or overnight on a rack in the refrigerator; this allows moisture to be drawn from the steak and then reabsorbed to concentrate the flavor. At this point, sprinkle both sides of steak with ribeye steak seasoning liberally.

Preheat a stovetop cast-iron grill or skillet to medium heat, add butter, and allow it to melt, coating it across the pan (or you can fry the steak without butter or oil). Cook for 3½ to 4 minutes per side depending on your desired doneness; remove steak and place onto a cutting board. Allow to stand for 5 minutes to become nice and juicy; cut across the grain for a tender bite and serve with your favorite salad or veggies.

---

*Choose your favorite steak: beef top sirloin, ribeye, chuck eye, flat iron

ON THE SIDE

Vegan Vegetarian Gluten-Free Dairy-Free Paleo

Zucchini Sauté

Yields 2–4 servings

Ingredients
1 tablespoon Earth Balance Olive Oil Buttery Spread
1 whole zucchini, ends removed, cut in half-rounds
½ teaspoon Vegetable seasoning
2 cups spinach, roughly chopped
Pinch sea salt and ground pepper

Directions
Sauté zucchini and vegetable seasoning in butter in a skillet over medium heat for 5 minutes. Add spinach and sauté 1 minute, stirring frequently; serve and add a pinch of sea salt and pepper.

Vegan Vegetarian Gluten-Free Dairy-Free Paleo

Roasted Herb'd Tomatoes

Yields 2–4 servings

Ingredients
2 vine-ripened tomatoes
1 tablespoon olive oil
2 garlic cloves, sliced
2 tablespoons fresh thyme leaves*
¼ teaspoon sea salt
⅛ teaspoon ground pepper

Directions
Core and cut tomatoes in half. Place right-side up onto a baking sheet and drizzle with olive oil, garlic, thyme leaves, sea salt, and pepper.

Roast in a preheated oven at 425°F for 20 to 25 minutes; remove from oven and serve.

*A variety of fresh herbs can be substituted: marjoram, rosemary, sage—the more the better!

Armenian Ikra

Yields 2–4 servings

Recipe inspired by my friend Adelina Nazaryan from Los Angeles.

Ingredients

½ yellow onion
1 large eggplant, pierced with fork
1 orange bell pepper*
1 yellow bell pepper
2 large whole elephant garlic cloves, skins on

1 vine-ripened tomato
2 tablespoons Earth Balance Olive Oil
　　Buttery Spread
1 teaspoon sea salt
¼–½ teaspoon Aleppo pepper flakes

Directions

Skewer onion, eggplant, garlic, and peppers. Preheat barbecue grill to 300°F and gently place the skewered veggies on the grill; close lid and grill for 20 minutes. Lift lid and gently rotate skewered veggies with barbecue utensils or mitts; continue to grill for an additional 20 minutes.

Remove veggies and allow to cool a bit. Remove veggies from skewers and peel them over a large bowl to capture remaining juices. Remove seeds and stems and roughly chop the veggies, reserving all juices.

Pour all veggies, along with juices, into a saucepan with butter and sea salt; stir and cook over medium heat for 5 minutes. Place handheld mixer into the saucepan and blend to your desired consistency; top with Aleppo pepper flakes and stir. Traditionally served with barbequed meat or toasted pita bread.

---

*Change your peppers and change your flavors and colors; try long green jalapenos and red bell peppers.

Vegan   Vegetarian   Gluten-Free   Dairy-Free   Paleo

Roasted Roots & Fresh Herbs

Yields 2–4 servings

Ingredients

5 carrots
2 small, thin parsnips
1 turnip
½ red onion
1½ tablespoons olive oil
½ teaspoon fresh rosemary leaves
1 teaspoon fresh thyme leaves

1 teaspoon fresh marjoram leaves
4 whole garlic cloves, smashed or minced
¼ teaspoon sea salt
Pinch ground pepper
Garnish with fresh thyme, rosemary, or
   sage sprigs

Directions

Cut the ends off carrots, parsnips, and the turnip, and cut each in half and then lengthwise once or twice until you have ½-inch matchsticks. Cut onion in desired pieces; set aside. Place vegetables and all other ingredients into a large bowl and coat well.

Place roots and herbs, except onion, onto a baking sheet and roast in a preheated oven at 425°F for 40 to 45 minutes, tossing once or twice while roasting. Add onions to the roasting roots during the last 20 to 25 minutes. The onions will caramelize and blacken if cooked too long, so keep an eye on those pups.

Toss roasted roots, onion, and herb scrapings into a bowl and sprinkle with sea salt and pepper; garnish with fresh herbs.

Pear & Walnut Arugula with White Balsamic Drizzle

Yields 2 servings

Ingredients

2 cups arugula
1 crisp Honey Belle pear, sliced lengthwise*
¼ cup walnuts

½ teaspoon sesame seeds
1–2 tablespoons 25 Star White Balsamic Vinegar**
½–1 teaspoon lemon, juiced

Directions

Arrange arugula onto a serving dish, then layer pear slices and drizzle a bit of lemon juice over the top to prevent oxidation; top with walnuts and sesame seeds. Drizzle balsamic over the top just before serving.

Note: If balsamic is too strong for your taste, whisk 1 part balsamic with 1 to 2 parts olive oil.

---

*Cut pears just prior consuming to limit oxidation.
**Fig balsamic vinegar also pairs well with this salad.

Vegetarian   Gluten-Free   Dairy-Free   Paleo

Omega Greens
with Pomegranate Drizzle

Yields 2–4 servings

Ingredients

2 cups organic fresh herb salad mix*
10 dandelion greens
1 avocado, sliced
1–2 organic pasture-raised Boiled Eggs,
  wedge cut (see page 271)

½ teaspoon flax seed
1–2 tablespoons pomegranate balsamic
  vinegar

Directions

Arrange salad mix, dandelions, avocado, egg, and flax onto a serving dish. Drizzle balsamic over the top just before serving.

Note: If balsamic is too strong for your taste, whisk 1 part balsamic with 1 to 2 parts olive oil.

---

*Fresh herb salad mix contains baby lettuces (red and green romaine, red and green oak leaf, red leaf, Lollo Rosso, Tango lettuce, red and green chard, etc.)

Vegan

Vegetarian

Gluten-Free

Dairy-Free

Coconut Jasmine Rice

Yields 2–4 servings

Ingredients
1 cup Organic Jasmine Rice by Lotus Foods
1½ cups coconut milk
Pinch sea salt

Directions
Combine all ingredients in a saucepan and bring to a boil. Cover, reduce heat, and simmer for 20 minutes. Fluff with fork and serve.

Watermelon Feta
& Strawberry Balsamic Drizzle

Yields 2–4 servings

Ingredients
1 cup arugula
3¼ cups watermelon, chopped
¾ cup cherry tomatoes, sliced*
1 full, thin sliver red onion, separated and sliced
⅛ cup feta, crumbled
⅛ teaspoon black pepper
1 tablespoon strawberry balsamic vinegar

Directions
Arrange arugula, watermelon, tomatoes, and onion onto a serving dish, sprinkle pepper and crumbled feta. Drizzle balsamic over the top and serve.

*Use a variety of colorful tomatoes; red, yellow, orange.

Vegan   Vegetarian   Gluten-Free   Dairy-Free   Paleo

Balsamic Beetroot Drizzle

Yields 4 servings

Ingredients
2 beets
3 large garlic cloves
Large pinch sea salt and pepper
1 tablespoon olive oil
4 fresh thyme sprigs
3 fresh rosemary sprigs
1 oregano sprig
1 marjoram sprig
1 tablespoon 25 Star White Balsamic Vinegar

Directions
Rinse and scrub beets and cut into sixths. Toss in a bowl with garlic, sea salt, pepper, oil, and balsamic; mix thoroughly. Wrap beets with drippings from remaining oil and balsamic in a large thick piece of foil. Roast in a preheated oven at 400°F for 45 minutes to 1 hour. Add fresh herb sprigs halfway through the roast, reseal foil, and continue roasting until beets are fork-tender.

Furikake String Beans

Yields 2–4 servings

Ingredients
¼ cup coconut aminos
1 teaspoon sesame oil
¼ teaspoon onion powder
⅛ teaspoon ginger powder
2 teaspoons Furikake Seasoning (see page 273)
3 tablespoons peanut oil
Handful fresh string beans

Directions
Combine coconut aminos, sesame oil, onion powder, ginger powder, and Furikake Seasoning in a small saucepan; simmer for 5 minutes to make furikake sauce.

In a small skillet sauté string beans in peanut oil for 3 minutes, pour furikake sauce over the top, and turn off the heat; toss a bit and use tongs to remove string beans onto a serving platter. Pour sauce into a small dish for dipping.

DESSERTS

Hawaiian Hurricane Popcorn with Furikake

Yields 4 servings

Ingredients for popcorn

1 cup organic corn kernels
¼ cup macadamia or coconut oil
¼ cup sesame seeds
1 tablespoon coconut sugar

1 teaspoon sea salt
2 nori sheets
¼ cup Furikake Seasoning

Directions

Preheat macadamia oil in a large saucepan on low-medium heat, then add 3 corn kernels and cover.

When the kernels pop, remove the lid; remove the saucepan from the heat; discard the 3 popped kernels. Pour the cup of kernels into the pot, cover, and put the pot back onto the heated burner for 2 to 3 minutes. When the kernels slow their pop cycle, remove the lid. Remove the pot from the heat, and set aside. Store unused popcorn in a paper bag for up to 3 days.

Now for the furikake: Toast sesame seeds in a dry cast iron skillet over low-medium heat for 3 minutes, stirring occasionally; set aside to cool. Make sure the skillet is not too hot as this will make the sesame seeds pop out of the skillet.

Cut your nori into small pieces and place into a food processor. Add coconut sugar, sea salt, and the cooled sesame seeds. Pulse until blended and place into a 4-ounce Mason jar in the refrigerator.

Pour 2 cups popped corn and ¼ cup Furikake Seasoning into a large glass bowl; cover with lid or tight plastic wrap and shake vigorously. Love butter? Use a couple tablespoons of melted Earth Balance Olive Oil Buttery Spread, toss, and enjoy.

Saffron Infused Coconut Cookies

Yields 2 servings

Ingredients

1 cup almond flour, sifted
¼ cup macaroon coconut
¼ cup saffron white chocolate, chopped*
1 teaspoon almond extract
½ teaspoon baking powder
⅓ cup coconut sugar
2 tablespoons coconut oil melted
2 tablespoons Autumn Applesauce (see page 73)
Garnish with a sprinkle of fine macaroon coconut powder (optional)

Directions

Mix all ingredients in a large bowl. Scoop 1 to 2 tablespoons of cookie dough and layer a baking sheet; each cookie should be 2 inches apart. Bake in a preheated oven at 375°F for 10 minutes for chewy cookies. Sprinkle coconut over the top while warm.

---

*Organic Saffron White Chocolate can be purchased at www.spicely.com. After going to Spicely's website, type in "Saffron White Chocolate" in the search box located to the upper-left. Or you can use your choice of chocolate chips.

Peanut Butter Cups

Yields 4–6 mini cup servings

Ingredients

¼ cup cacao butter*
¼ cup cacao powder
1 tablespoon maple syrup
1 teaspoon alcohol-free vanilla extract
2 tablespoons Toasted Honey Peanut Butter, divided (see page 267)
4 large cupcake paper liners or 6 mini cupcake paper liners

Directions

Fill a small saucepan with ¼ cup chunks of cacao butter and simmer until melted. Turn off heat and whisk in cacao powder, maple syrup, and vanilla extract until completely dissolved. Place 4 cupcake paper liners into a cupcake tray and spoon a thin layer of melted chocolate sauce into the bottom of each liner. Dollop and divide peanut butter into the center and fill with the remaining chocolate sauce. Place tray in the refrigerator for up to 2 hours. Remove from the refrigerator, peel away the paper cup, and devour!

---

*Raw Cacao Butter from The Raw Food World was used in this recipe. It can be purchased on Amazon if not found in your local market.

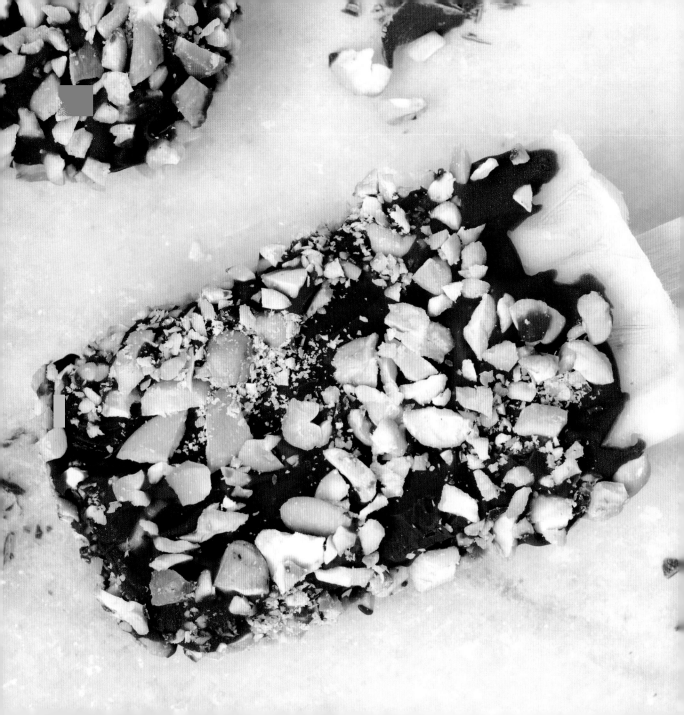

Magic Shell Coconut Cream Pie Pops

Yields 6 servings

Ingredients for Coconut Cream Pie
½ frozen banana
1 teaspoon maca
½ cup coconut water
⅛ teaspoon fresh ginger, minced
1 tablespoon vanilla protein powder
¼ cup fresh young Thai coconut meat*
½ cup coconut milk
8 coconut milk ice cubes
2 tablespoons agave

Ingredients for Magic Shell**
3 tablespoons coconut oil, melted
2 tablespoons cocoa powder
1 tablespoon maple syrup
Garnish with chopped peanuts (not paleo)

Continued on next page

---

*Fresh young Thai coconut water and coconut meat are best used straight from the coconut; alternatively, you can purchase Thai coconut meat in the freezer aisle of your local market and use bottled coconut water.

**To create a thicker, richer dark chocolatey Magic Shell, use 2 tablespoons melted coconut oil, 3 tablespoons cocoa powder, and 1 tablespoon maple syrup as an alternative.

Directions

Let's start by creating the pops. Blend all coconut cream pie ingredients in a high speed blender for 40 seconds or until smooth. Pour into ice pop trays and freeze for 1 hour. Insert popsicle sticks and continue to freeze until frozen solid, at least 4 hours.

Now for the fun part, making the Magic Shell. Combine melted coconut oil, cocoa powder, and maple syrup into a small coffee mug and whisk thoroughly until creamy. Remove the popsicles from the freezer and run them under hot water for a few seconds until the pops can be removed easily. Dip each pop into the melted Magic Shell in the coffee mug, swirl it around a bit to coat it well, and sprinkle with chopped peanuts. Set aside to see—10, 20, 30 seconds—the magic happen! Now devour those puppies!

Banana Nut Bread

Yields 6 servings

Ingredients

1½ cup organic unbleached all-purpose flour
1 teaspoon baking soda
½ teaspoon sea salt
½ cup pecans, chopped
½ teaspoon cinnamon
3 bananas, ripened and peeled
1½ teaspoon alcohol-free vanilla extract

½ cup Autumn Applesauce (see page 73)
½ cup maple syrup
⅓ cup canned organic coconut milk
1 organic pasture-raised egg
1 tablespoon Earth Balance Olive Oil Buttery Spread for greasing*
½ cup walnuts, for topping

Directions

Sift flour, baking soda, and salt into a bowl and set aside. Dry roast pecans and cinnamon in a small skillet for 5 minutes, tossing occasionally, set aside.

In a separate bowl combine bananas, vanilla, applesauce, maple syrup, and coconut milk; smash with a potato masher or fork thoroughly. Whisk in egg with a fork, then add roasted pecans and cinnamon, and slowly stir in the flour mixture until well blended. Be sure not to overmix or the bread will become dense.

Grease 9x5x3-inch glass loaf pan with butter and pour in banana nut bread mixture; top with walnuts. Bake in preheated oven at 350°F for 30 to 35 minutes.

Allow to cool and remove banana nut bread from the loaf pan; slice and enjoy with a slather of butter and honey, if desired.

*Earth Balance Olive Oil Buttery Spread can be replaced with coconut oil.

Gooey Macadamia Treats

Yields 6 servings

Ingredients
½ cup macadamia nuts
3 Medjool dates, pitted
¼ cup dried cherries
1 tablespoon honey
1 tablespoon chia seeds
¼ cup coconut flakes

Directions
Soak macadamia nuts, Medjool dates, and dried cherries for 30 minutes; drain and add to a small food processor, then pulse for 20 seconds until well blended. Add honey and chia seeds; pulse for another 15 seconds.

Spoon 1 tablespoon of mixture into your hands and form into balls; roll over coconut flakes and enjoy.

Vegan   Vegetarian   Gluten-Free   Dairy-Free   Paleo

Mochi Puffs

Yields 4 servings

Ingredients

4 (1-inch) pieces of Grainaissance Mochi*
Garnish with your favorite combinations: GO VEGGIE Vegan Classic Plain Cream Cheese and brown rice syrup, Earth Balance Organic Coconut Spread, or drizzled with brown rice syrup. Wrap a thin layer of nori (seaweed) around your puff.

Directions

Cut mochi into 1-inch squares with a sharp knife and place each piece onto a baking sheet 1 inch apart. Bake in a preheated oven at 450°F for 8 minutes or until you see them puff up like little marshmallows. Remove from oven and allow to cool. Snack on them plain or choose your favorite garnish combinations.

Author's Note: Carefully pierce a hole on the side of your Mochi Puff and stuff with GO VEGGIE cream cheese and a drizzle of brown rice syrup or garnish with any of your favorite combinations; be creative.

*Grainaissance Mochi can be found at www.grainaissance.com/mochi; cinnamon and raisin or other flavors are available.

Vegan Vegetarian Gluten-Free Dairy-Free Paleo

Blueberry Goji Pudding

Yields 1 serving

Ingredients
1 cup almond milk
½ cup fresh blueberries
1 tablespoon honey
2 tablespoons dried goji berries
¼ cup chia seeds
Garnish with mint sprigs and a dash of cinnamon (optional)

Directions
Blend almond milk, blueberries, and honey in a high speed blender for 40 seconds. Pour into a Mason jar and add goji berries and chia seeds, then gently stir. Set aside for 10–15 minutes, then refrigerate for up to 3 hours or overnight for it to thicken; garnish with mint and cinnamon.

Vegan

Vegetarian

Gluten-Free

Dairy-Free

Paleo

Coconut Key Lime Pie Cup

Yields 2 servings

Ingredients
½ cup pecans
7 dates, pitted and diced
1 teaspoon cacao powder
2 tablespoons agave plus 1 teaspoon agave
1 cup coconut cream*
⅛ cup key lime juice (approx. 3 key limes)
1 teaspoon alcohol-free vanilla extract
Garnish with 1 teaspoon lime zest (optional)

Directions
Let's start with the crust. Place pecans in a small food processor; pulse nuts until small and crumbly. Toss in diced dates; pulse until the mixture becomes gooey. Then sprinkle in the cacao powder and drizzle 1 teaspoon agave; pulse until the mixture is dark, chocolatey, and fluffy. Do not over process; that can cause the crust to become too buttery.

Continued on next page

---

*You may use 1 can organic coconut milk where the only ingredients are coconut, water and guar gum. Each can contains approximately 1 cup coconut cream. Keep the can in the coldest part of the refrigerator until use. Do not shake can or the cream and liquid will emulsify. We want to keep it separated. After opening, carefully scoop the cream from the top of the can and reserve the liquid for smoothies.

Divide the mixture and gently press into the bottom of two small glasses or two 4-ounce Mason jars; cover and refrigerate while making the key lime filling.

Now for the coconut key lime pie filling. Blend coconut cream, lime juice, vanilla, and 2 tablespoons agave in a large mixing bowl with an electric mixer until there are light and fluffy peaks of cream.

Remove the Mason jars from the refrigerator and gently spoon and divide the coconut key lime pie filling over the crust; top with lime zest and refrigerate for at least 2 hours. Remove from the refrigerator, get two little spoons, and make sure you share this all raw vegan goodness!

Garnish ideas: a sprinkle of coconut sugar or macaroon coconut flakes

Blueberry Mousse & Coconut Cream

Yields 2 servings

Ingredients
1 cup blueberries, fresh or frozen
¼ cup coconut sugar
¼ cup Greek God Plain Kefir
¼ cup GO VEGGIE Vegan Classic Plain Cream Cheese
1 cup coconut cream*
1 teaspoon alcohol-free vanilla extract
2 tablespoons agave

Directions
Cook blueberries and coconut sugar in a small saucepan on low for 10 minutes; stirring occasionally until you've obtained a blueberry syrup. Remove from heat and allow to cool.

Continued on next page

---

*You may use 1 can organic coconut milk where the only ingredients are coconut, water, and guar gum. Each can contains approximately 1 cup coconut cream. Keep the can in the coldest part of the refrigerator until use. Do not shake can or the cream and liquid will emulsify. We want to keep it separated. After opening, carefully scoop the cream from the top of the can and reserve the liquid for smoothies.

Combine milk kefir and cream cheese into a food processor and blend thoroughly to create a sour cream. Pour the slightly cooled blueberry syrup over the sour cream in the food processor and blend until silky. Spoon into desired serving glasses and refrigerate to set while making the coconut cream topping.

Now for the good stuff! Extremely addicting sweetened coconut cream. Blend coconut cream, vanilla, and agave in a large mixing bowl with an electric mixer until there are light and fluffy peaks of cream. Remove blueberry mousse from the refrigerator and spoon the coconut cream over the top. Eat immediately or refrigerate until it's time for dessert.

Pomberry Ice Cream

Yields 4–6 servings

Ingredients

2 cups frozen strawberries*
2 cups pomegranate seeds, juiced (approx. 6 ounces or ¾ cup juice)**
2 tablespoons agave
½ teaspoon alcohol-free vanilla extract
¾ cup coconut cream***

Directions

Place all ingredients in a high speed blender and blend for 48 seconds. Pour into a glass bowl and freeze for 1 hour. Remove from freezer, scoop into cute little paper cups, and serve immediately.

---

*Hull strawberries before freezing.

**Pomegranate seeds can be purchased in the frozen section of most local markets. 2 cups pomegranate seeds juiced yields 6 ounces of juice. Bottled pomegranate juice can be substituted; only 100 percent pure, not from concentrate and no added sugar or preservatives.

***You may use 1 can organic coconut milk where the ingredients are only coconut, water, and guar gum. Each can contains approximately 1 cup coconut cream. Keep the can in the coldest part of the refrigerator until use. Do not shake can or the cream and liquid will emulsify. We want to keep it separated. After opening, carefully scoop the cream from the top of the can and reserve the liquid for smoothies.

SAUCES, DIPS & MORE

Vegan-opt Vegetarian-opt Gluten-Free Dairy-Free-opt Paleo-opt

Tzatziki Dipping Sauce

Yields 2–4 servings

Ingredients
¼ cup Greek God Plain Kefir*
¼ cup GO VEGGIE Vegan Classic Plain Cream Cheese
1 large garlic clove
¼ teaspoon sea salt
1 teaspoon lime juice
½ teaspoon Tzatziki seasoning
3-inch length English cucumber, diced and divided
2 tablespoons fresh dill, chopped and divided

Directions
Combine milk kefir, cream cheese, garlic, sea salt, lime juice, Tzatziki seasoning, half the diced cucumbers, and half the fresh dill into a food processor and pulse approximately 6 to 7 times to mix, leaving it a bit chunky.

Pour Tzatziki into a serving bowl and top with the remaining cucumber and dill; refrigerate to chill before serving.

---

*Coconut Milk Yogurt can be substituted for those who have a strong dairy intolerance (see page 257).

Vegan   Vegetarian   Gluten-Free   Dairy-Free   Paleo

Coconut Milk Yogurt

Yields 4 cups

Ingredients
1 fresh young Thai coconut*
2 teaspoons probiotic powder**

Directions
Open the young Thai coconut and pour the coconut water into a high speed blender. Scoop out all of the soft coconut meat and place it in the blender with the coconut water.

Blend in a high speed blender for 45 seconds until creamy; pour into a clean dry Mason jar. Use a non-metal spoon to stir in probiotic powder; cover with a piece of cheese cloth and secure with a rubber band.

Place the Mason jar in the oven, turn on the oven light and allow to set for 24 hours. Within those 24 hours, the liquid will expand; this means the living organisms are thriving and creating beneficial bacteria. The coconut milk yogurt can now be refrigerated for a few hours, then consumed. Try topping it with a bit of honey, maple syrup, or agave with fresh fruit and nuts for a special treat!

Continued on next page

*1 fresh young Thai coconut yields approximately 1½ cups coconut water and ½ cup coconut meat; use everything you can get out of the coconut.
**Solaray Multidophilus Powder (non-dairy, freeze-dried, 5 billion triple strain formula): keep this product stored in the refrigerator.

Author's note: Can't find any coconuts? No problem. Nothing will taste as good as using a fresh coconut, but there are alternatives.

Exotic Superfood Young Thai 100% raw coconut meat can be purchased in the frozen section of your local market; allow coconut meat to thaw on counter to room temperature before use. Bottled coconut water can also be substituted, but be sure there are no added sugars or preservatives.

Want a quick way to open your coconut in just seconds? I love my Coco-Jack! One investment that keeps on giving. Just go to www.coco-jack.com, place your order, and type INDULGE in the coupon code box.

Coconut milk yogurt tends to have a lighter consistency than Greek God Plain Kefir; therefore, when using coconut milk yogurt for Tzatziki Dipping Sauce, reduce the amount of garlic.

Vegan Vegetarian Gluten-Free Dairy-Free

Thai Peanut Sauce

Yields 4–6 servings

Ingredients
2 small garlic cloves, minced
Pinch sea salt
2 teaspoons olive oil
¼ cup coconut aminos
¼ cup organic low-sodium vegetable broth
2 tablespoons Toasted Honey Peanut Butter (see page 267)
Garnish with 1 teaspoon crushed peanuts (optional)

Directions:
Sauté garlic and salt in oil for 2 minutes until golden brown; add broth and coconut aminos, then bring to a boil. Cook for 5 minutes, stirring occasionally. Reduce heat to a low boil and add peanut butter; cook at a low boil for 2½ to 3 minutes, stirring frequently while the sauce thickens. Pour into a small dish and top with crushed peanuts; allow to cool thoroughly before dipping.

Homemade Sour Cream

Yields 2–4 servings

Ingredients
½ cup GO VEGGIE Vegan Classic Plain Cream Cheese
½ cup Greek Gods Plain Kefir*

Directions
Combine GO VEGGIE cream cheese and milk kefir in a bowl and whisk thoroughly; store in a glass container in the refrigerator for up to a week.

---

*Coconut Milk Yogurt can be substituted for those who have a strong dairy intolerance (see page 257).

Dynamite Pico De Gallo

Yields 2 cups

Ingredients
⅓ cup red or white onion, diced
⅓ cup cilantro, chopped
2–3 tomatoes, diced*
1 garlic clove, minced
1 red Thai pepper, diced, stem and seeds removed**
½ lime, juiced
⅛ teaspoon sea salt

Directions
Combine all ingredients into a serving bowl, toss a bit; refrigerate for a few hours to infuse flavors, then devour.

---

*Roma or plum tomatoes work best, meatier and less liquid
**Serrano or jalapeno pepper can be substituted; red jalapenos work great if you want less heat.

Vegan

Vegetarian

Gluten-Free

Dairy-Free

Paleo

Blueberry Jam

Yields 2–4 servings

Ingredients
1 cup fresh blueberries
¼ cup coconut sugar
1 tablespoon chia seeds

Directions
Combine all ingredients in a small saucepan and cook on low for 15 minutes, stirring occasionally. Be sure to set your timer. During the first 8 to 10 minutes, use a silicone spatula to smash a few berries and stir as you see the liquid form into a syrup. During the last 5 minutes, the syrup will thicken and slightly start to bubble; stir more frequently at this point.

While piping hot, pour blueberry jam into a 4-ounce Mason jar and seal with a lid. Allow to cool a bit on the countertop before it is devoured or placed in the refrigerator.

Toasted Honey Peanut Butter

Yields 4–6 servings

Ingredients

1½ cups raw shelled peanuts
¼ cup olive or peanut oil

2 teaspoons honey*
¼ scant teaspoon sea salt

Directions

Dry toast raw peanuts in a nonstick skillet over medium-low heat for approximately 8 minutes, tossing occasionally so peanuts don't burn. This allows the peanuts to sweat out natural oils. If the peanuts start to blacken too quickly or pop in the skillet, turn down the heat to achieve a slow toast.

Transfer toasted peanuts into a high speed blender for a smooth peanut butter or food processor for a chunkier consistency. Blend for 30 seconds, then add oil. Continue to blend 30 more seconds. Add honey and sea salt and continue to blend for 30 more seconds. Use a spatula to scrape the mixture back to the bottom of the blender, if necessary.

Continue this process for up to a total of 5 minutes. Then you will see the magic happen: a natural toasted honey peanut butter so good you'll be eating it with a spoon.

Use a silicone spatula to scrape the peanut butter into a 4-ounce Mason jar. Place lid and store in the refrigerator for up to a month. It can also be stored in the cupboard; oils may separate over time, so give it a little whirl with your spoon before consuming.

---

*Vegan option: maple syrup

Vegan   Vegetarian   Gluten-Free   Dairy-Free   Paleo

Vegetable Broth

Yields 6+ servings

Ingredients

2 cups yellow onion
1 cup carrots
1 cup celery
1 cup parsnip
1 cup white potatoes
1 cup sweet potato
1 cup baby bella mushrooms
6 cups water
1 teaspoon sea salt
½ teaspoon dill

½ teaspoon marjoram
½ teaspoon rosemary
½ teaspoon crushed peppercorn
1 teaspoon parsley
1 teaspoon thyme
1 bay leaf
1 teaspoon savory leaves
6 ounces (¾ cup) fresh Honeycrisp apple
   juice

Directions

Chop all vegetables into 2-inch pieces and place in a large saucepan along with all other ingredients. Bring to a boil, reduce heat, cover, and simmer for 2 hours.

Line a strainer with 2 layers of cheesecloth and strain broth into a Mason jar. Seal and refrigerate for up to 5 days or freeze until used; allow to cool before placing into the freezer.

Discard veggies or eat them with a dollop of Earth Balance Olive Oil Buttery Spread and a pinch of sea salt and pepper.

Vegan   Vegetarian   Gluten-Free   Dairy-Free   Paleo

Red Pepper Paste

Yields 6+ servings

Recipe inspired by my friend Adelina Nazaryan from Los Angeles.

Ingredients
30 red jalapeno peppers
1 teaspoon sea salt
⅛ cup olive oil

Directions
Remove and discard stems and most of the seeds from red jalapenos. Grind jalapeno peppers in a food processor and purée into a mash. (Remaining chunks and pieces give texture to the paste.) Use a silicone spatula to scrape jalapeno mash into a small saucepan; add sea salt and stir. Bring to a low simmering bubble, reduce heat to low and cook uncovered for 2 hours until the consistency is a bit like ketchup, stirring occasionally; set aside and allow to cool.

Spread red pepper mixture onto a dehydrator tray and cook at 115°F for 3⅓ hours. The mixture will turn into a paste-like texture. Scrape all the chili paste into a 6-ounce Mason jar, making sure to pack it down to eliminate bubbles. Pour olive oil over the top, secure the lid, and refrigerate.

Author's note: Want to spice up your red pepper paste? Try a combination of one or two flavorful add-ins (just stir them with the mash during the simmer): Aleppo pepper flakes, lemon juice, garlic, cumin, chipotle, cayenne, sun-dried tomatoes, and sweet or smoky paprika. This basic and versatile red pepper paste recipe will enhance any dish.

Vegetarian

Gluten-Free

Dairy-Free

Paleo

Boiled Eggs

Yields 6 servings

Ingredients
6 brown organic pasture-raised eggs

Directions
In a small saucepan, add eggs and enough water to rise ½ inch above the eggs. Bring to a boil and reduce heat to a low boil for 10 minutes. While eggs are cooking, make an ice bath by putting a tray of ice cubes into a large bowl of cold water.

Remove one egg at a time from the heat with a slotted spoon and place them into the prepared ice bath immediately. Allow eggs to cool; arrange boiled eggs in egg carton and refrigerate until used.

Vegetarian

Gluten-Free

Dairy-Free

Paleo

Poached Eggs

Yields 1–4 servings

Ingredients
1–4 organic pasture-raised eggs
1 teaspoon white balsamic vinegar
Garnish with a pinch of sea salt, pepper, dill, or other herbs (optional)

Directions
In a very small skillet or saucepan, fill with water approximately 2 inches deep. Bring the water to a boil, then reduce to a low boil. Gently pour 1 egg into a small ramekin. Add white balsamic vinegar to the water, and whirl the water and vinegar in a circular motion.

Gently pour the egg into the center of the skillet. Use a slotted spoon and gently swirl the water around the outer portion of the egg to keep it intact. Cook for 3 minutes, then use a slotted spoon to gently lift the egg out of the water. Allow the water to seep through the slots of the spoon and place onto a serving dish. Add a pinch of sea salt, pepper, dill, or your favorite herbs.

When making multiple poached eggs, do not overcrowd the eggs; they should not be touching.

Vegan   Vegetarian   Gluten-Free   Dairy-Free   Paleo

Furikake Seasoning

Yields 4 ounces

Ingredients
¼ cup sesame seeds, white or black or a combination
1 tablespoon coconut sugar
1 teaspoon sea salt
2 nori sheets

Directions
Toast sesame seeds in a dry cast iron skillet over low-medium heat for 3 minutes, stirring occasionally; set aside to cool. Make sure the skillet is not too hot as this will burn the sesame seeds and they will pop out of the skillet.

Cut nori into small pieces and place into a food processor. Add coconut sugar, sea salt, and the cooled sesame seeds. Pulse until blended; store unused Furikake Seasoning in a 4-ounce Mason jar in the refrigerator until use.

Vegan

Vegetarian

Gluten-Free

Dairy-Free

Paleo

Sweet & Hot Jalapenos

Ingredients
5 jalapenos, sliced
3 garlic cloves
2 pinches crushed peppercorn
½ teaspoon whole coriander seeds
1 tablespoon fresh dill sprigs
1 teaspoon sea salt
1 tablespoon maple syrup
½ cup water
½ cup white balsamic vinegar

Directions
Layer jalapenos, garlic, peppercorn, coriander seeds, and dill sprigs in 4-ounce Mason jar; set aside.

Combine salt, maple syrup, water, and vinegar in a small saucepan and boil for 2 minutes, stirring constantly. Gently pour over the jalapenos into the Mason jar, filling it to the top; cover and press down the center of the lid while securing the ring. Allow to cool on the countertop before refrigerating. Perfect for pizza toppings, sandwiches, spicing up jambalaya, and so much more!

References

Sources that were influential in the writing and researching of this book include:

Cherries
http://www.lifeextension.com/Magazine/2007/12/sf_cherries/Page-01

Understanding Free Radicals and Antioxidants
http://www.healthchecksystems.com/antioxid.htm

Phytic Acid in Food
http://www.phyticacid.org/

Is Honey More Effective Than Cough Medicine?
http://articles.mercola.com/sites/articles/archive/2007/12/22/is-honey-more-effective-than-cough-medicine.aspx

Testimonials

"Michelle understands how to combine foods to create the wow factor. Her smoothies are nutritionally dense, flavorful, and beautifully presented. She truly has a gift."

—Melissa Kubek

liteBOD Health & Energy, litebod.com

"Michelle's recipes are so full of life that your body and taste buds will think you're having a party. They are easy to prepare even for the novice cook, like me, and are a treat for the whole family. They make a vegan lifestyle simple to adopt. When Michelle cooks, you can feel the love in each bite and even when you make the recipes yourself, the love comes through. Thank you with all my heart, Michelle."

—Sunita Shinde

"Michelle is amazing at putting together tastes and food designs! She has a natural ability to make the tastebuds wake up, and her foods are a culinary delight and healthy too!"

—Karen Brake

"I had tried everything to lose weight and feel better, to no avail. Then Michelle introduced me to juicing and a healthier way of eating. I have lost a considerable amount of weight, and I feel terrific for the first time in a long time. And I don't feel deprived at all. Most people don't realize there are a lot of healthy foods that are just as satisfying and don't pack the pounds on. There are no fast and easy ways to lose weight. It has to be a lifestyle change. Michelle has taught me so much about combining the right foods and just what to eat to help with weightloss. And I've kept it off, too.

"Michelle's recipes are always fast and easy to make. The best thing about her recipes, though, is they offer something new and different instead of eating the same old thing. She has introduced me to so many different foods that I never would have tried on my own, and she explains what each food does for your body. Finally, interesting recipes that are good for your body and that taste great."

—Carol Paradise

"My wife and I used to eat whatever we wanted and felt high and low and sleepy after a food coma. Now that we're in the process of following The Green Aisle detox, we feel more focused with choices in life, at work and with our baby. Wc both sleep easier and feel that we can wake up without snoozing the alarm anymore. Thank you!"

—Hovo and Adelina Nazaryan

"As a health coach I'm always looking for healthy material to recommend to my clients and this book definitely supports good health! In the beginning, this book has some great information on healthy eating and food in general. Then, dive into some great recipes that will refresh and you healthy! I give this book to all of the clients in my program, highly recommend it!"

—Steven Loeschner, Steve Loeschner LLC, steveloeschner.com

Index

Conversion Charts

Metric and Imperial Conversions
(These conversions are rounded for convenience)

Ingredient	Cups/Tablespoons/ Teaspoons	Ounces	Grams/Milliliters
Butter	1 cup=16 tablespoons=2 sticks	8 ounces	230 grams
Cream cheese	1 tablespoon	0.5 ounce	14.5 grams
Cheese, shredded	1 cup	4 ounces	110 grams
Cornstarch	1 tablespoon	0.3 ounce	8 grams
Flour, all-purpose	1 cup/1 tablespoon	4.5 ounces/0.3 ounce	125 grams/8 grams
Flour, whole wheat	1 cup	4 ounces	120 grams
Fruit, dried	1 cup	4 ounces	120 grams
Fruits or veggies, chopped	1 cup	5 to 7 ounces	145 to 200 grams
Fruits or veggies, puréed	1 cup	8.5 ounces	245 grams
Honey, maple syrup, or corn syrup	1 tablespoon	.75 ounce	20 grams
Liquids: cream, milk, water, or juice	1 cup	8 fluid ounces	240 milliliters
Oats	1 cup	5.5 ounces	150 grams
Salt	1 teaspoon	0.2 ounce	6 grams
Spices: cinnamon, cloves, ginger, or nutmeg (ground)	1 teaspoon	0.2 ounce	5 milliliters
Sugar, brown, firmly packed	1 cup	7 ounces	200 grams
Sugar, white	1 cup/1 tablespoon	7 ounces/0.5 ounce	200 grams/12.5 grams
Vanilla extract	1 teaspoon	0.2 ounce	4 grams

Oven Temperatures

Fahrenheit	Celsius	Gas Mark
225°	110°	¼
250°	120°	½
275°	140°	1
300°	150°	2
325°	160°	3
350°	180°	4
375°	190°	5
400°	200°	6
425°	220°	7
450°	230°	8